# THE
# SPARKLE
# TRAP

ISBN Hardcover: 979-8-9997733-0-2
ISBN Paperback: 979-8-9997733-3-3
ISBN E-book: 979-8-9997733-1-9

Cover design: Daniel de Llano

Interior design: Megan Sheer

# THE SPARKLE TRAP

Recognizing, "Escaping," and Healing from
Narcissistic Abuse in LGBTQ+ Love

DANIEL DE LLANO

If you've received this book unexpectedly,

please consider whether it's an SOS from someone you love:

A quiet cry for support

An invitation to see the full picture of a sparkle trap.

With love,

Daniel

# FOREWORD

There are books that inform you, and there are books that transform you. From the very first page of The Sparkle Trap, I knew this was not merely a book about narcissistic relationships—it was a lifeline. It was a mirror held up with compassion, a hand extended in solidarity, and a pathway toward reclaiming the self you thought you lost. This work is not just about recognizing toxic patterns; it is about remembering your brilliance. It is a journey of returning to yourself—wiser, stronger, and more radiant than before.

I met Daniel as his coach, but over time, our connection deepened into a friendship built on authenticity, courage, and mutual respect. From the first conversation, I could feel his heart—genuine, loving, and fiercely committed to truth. What moved me most in his journey, and in this book, is his refusal to leave the reader in the place of pain. Yes, he exposes manipulation. Yes, he fearlessly names the behaviors that so many suffer in silence. But he does not stop there. He leads you into your liberation. He guides you beyond the trauma and into your power. His message is not one of blame—it is one of rebirth.

Many books on narcissistic abuse focus solely on the darkness: the manipulation, the confusion, the slow erosion of self-worth. But Daniel does something profoundly different. He honors your pain while reminding you of your strength. He names the cruelty without stripping you of dignity. He validates every tear, every silent scream, every moment of doubt—and then shows you how to rise from it. This book is a transmutation chamber, turning heartbreak into awakening, confusion into clarity, and helplessness into sovereignty. It reminds you that what happened to you is not a reflection of your weakness, but of your radiance. Narcissists are drawn to light—and if you are holding this book, it is because you have always been a light.

Daniel writes with a voice that is both angel and warrior. He knows this path intimately, not as an observer, but as someone who has walked through the fire and emerged with the keys to freedom. He does not speak at you; he walks with you. Every chapter feels like a conversation with someone who understands the depths of your pain but is equally committed to your expansion. He brings levity to heavy truths through humor and creativity, using language that disarms fear and makes complicated psychological concepts feel clear, approachable, and even empowering.

What makes this book extraordinary is its commitment to healing. Not surface-level healing, but true cellular, emotional, and spiritual liberation. Daniel goes beyond survival. He invites you into a higher destiny. Through his guidance, you will not only see the patterns that once held you captive—you will break them. You will reclaim your intuition. You will restore your boundaries. You will learn how to love again, not from a place of longing or fear, but from a place of sovereignty and joy. And most of all, you will remember that your sparkle was never lost—only temporarily covered.

If you have ever felt small in someone else's presence...

If you have questioned your worth, your sanity, or your reality...

If you have poured your love into someone who only consumed it while giving back confusion— know this: your story is not ending in pain. It is beginning in power. And this book is your turning point.

Daniel has given the world a masterpiece of truth and restoration. You will leave these pages not as a victim of your story, but as the author of a new one. The Sparkle Trap is not just a book—it is initiation. An initiation into the brilliance you were born with, the freedom you deserve, and the love that begins within you.

As you read these pages, I invite you to let them land in your heart. Take your time. Breathe between sentences. Feel the resonance. Let your nervous system know: you are safe now. You are seen. You are not broken—you are becoming.

And so, with great love, deep respect, and unwavering belief in your magnificence, I welcome you into this journey. May this book be the moment you remember who you are.

Your sparkle was never lost.

It has been waiting for this exact moment—for you to rise.

— Francesca Facio, Coach, Speaker and Author of *Unleash Your Wings* and *How to be Human in the Age of AI*

## Disclaimer #1

This book is a healing tool for the queer community. It is not a revenge tool. The stories shared are based on real-life experiences I've lived or collected from others, including:

Jon
Shannon
Jonnathan
Cori
Megan
Joe

So…

"I'm not telling the story of my ex."

**[Sound of books slamming shut]**

Also, all the names in this book are fake…

**[???]**

…including the ones listed above…

**[Sound of books slamming shut]**

…for identity protection.

## Disclaimer #2

For those who might be reading this book with intentions to harm…
This book might be a very uncomfortable mirror for you.
The world can be a beautiful place for you too.
Please, go pray. Meditate. Touch some grass.
Just don't read this book.
Thank you.
[ … ]

## Disclaimer #3

This is not a disclaimer …
Ok, fine, it is. But …
It's also a heartfelt note from someone who once felt like you:
This book is not a substitute for therapy, legal help, or emergency
support. If you think you need professional assistance, please —
make that call. You deserve care. Starting the healing process is
already a win. Find the version that works for you and take that
step.

**[Soft sound of people breathing, pausing to reflect]**

One day, I picked up my self-love from the floor,
and the scattered pieces of myself, and I said:

*I don't even care if my things end up on fire in Dolores Park ...
I'm now ready to leave.*

**With that huge wave of strength, rage, and (for the first time)
truly prioritizing myself, I left.**

I hope this book takes you to that moment... the one where you
*finally understand* that you should be Number One on your own
VIP list, and from there, onto a path of growth and healing that
finally brings you peace.

**Welcome to the other side of *The Sparkle Trap*.**

**For you, the one who was too radiant to go unnoticed**

Hi, love.

This isn't a course about narcissism. It's a journey back to the best version of yourself, waiting just a block away.

You're not here only to analyze the one who dimmed your light; you're here to understand what you went (or are going) through, and to gather resources to leave and heal from it.

You're here to remember why you shone so brightly that someone felt the urge to control you.

In the queer world, we've learned to survive, to adapt, to seduce, to read the room… and then, to navigate.

And it's exactly because we're intense, sexy, smart, exciting, and sensitive that some people choose us to feed their own safety by draining ours.

Let me tell you something important:

From now on…

- You don't need validation.

- You don't need to share your story with just anyone.

- You don't need to justify why it took time to leave; you were still figuring yourself out.

Don't cast pearls before swine. Your opinions, your perspective, and your story are pearls, and not everyone deserves them. Not everyone can understand you. Not everyone has lived what you've lived. Your story deserves to be told only when it serves your healing.

As a coach, I see this all the time: people trapped in the victim role. And yes, it can feel comforting. It brings quick attention. But it doesn't let us step into our full potential.

After what you've lived through, you are powerful. Capable. An example. A survivor. Not someone stuck in pain.

This journey we're about to take is not to dramatize your past or your present, but to understand it and heal from it, to rebuild your queer power, your intuition, your desire, and your boundaries so that you can love again without shrinking. And so that you never again confuse intensity with love.

Thank you for making it this far. For choosing yourself. For giving yourself another chance to be fully you. For giving me the opportunity to be here with you, in this vulnerable moment.

**Welcome home.**

With love, Daniel de Llano

In this book you will find terms like:

**Hold your unicorns** — Queer version of "Hold your horses."

**Info-Shield™** — The protective shield we create to contain damage by using information and evidence.

**PS's Classic Combos** — Combinations of different manipulation techniques used by the narcissist.

**Narci-Baptism™** — The act of assigning a new name to the narcissist.

**Narci-Strategic™** — The art of using smart tools against the elaborate games of toxic people.

**Narci-AI™** — Your new bestie: AI-powered clarity when their fog feels too real.

**Narci-Mantra™** — Short affirmations to rewire your brain and shut down their spell.

**Narci-Form™** — A structured set of questions that corner the narcissist and produce written proof.

**Narci-Questions™** — Questions designed to expose manipulation.

**Narci-Box™** — Your everyday toolbox against narcissists.

**Neuroplasticity** — The capacity of the brain to change how neurons connect, creating new habits and managing triggers.

**Rivian** — An American electric car.

**Spiralizing** — How a "sweet and confused Spaniard" (me) once said *spiraling*, generating smiles all around.

**Instructions for the reader:**

Many times in this book, the word *narcissist* or *your partner* will be replaced by **PS**. The goal is to get some distance from the person hurting us — to take power away from them and give it back to us.

**PS** can mean many things, so I want you to choose. Let me give you some examples for your reference:

- PS
- Putrid Sock
- Pompous Slug
- Pretentious Shrew
- Pompous Shit
- Pasty Sloth
- Pretend Sweetheart
- Pathetic Showman
- .........................................

Which one is the new name of... PS?

.............................. ...........

[**Narci-Baptism**™ completed]

Throughout this book, you'll find ♛**ACTION STEPS** at the end of each chapter. These are short, practical exercises designed to help you integrate what you've just read through reflection, journaling, or simple actions that reconnect you with your power.

You'll also find **QR CODES** at the end of each *section* of the book. They'll take you to extra resources: videos where we connect face to face, self-hypnosis audios, and other tools to deepen your healing. Think of them as bonus portals of support. You're not alone in the process, but guided and understood.

Healing can feel lonely, but I promise: through these steps and codes, you'll always have a voice (mine!) walking next to you.

I've prepared a welcome video where you can get to know me better (and get to hear my *"exotic"* accent LOL).

**So, simply scan the QR code below, and I'll see you on the other side!**

Advice: If you are not in a private or safe environment, please use headphones before scanning any QR codes in this book, or wait until you can safely access these resources.

If you cannot keep this book in a safe place, avoid writing in the journaling sections. Instead, use a journaling app or a private notebook, but please, *journal!* It is powerful, even if you don't believe that yet.

www.thesparkletrap.com/qr1

# THE MAP OUT OF THE TRAP

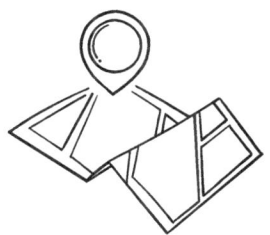

# GLUE REMOVER

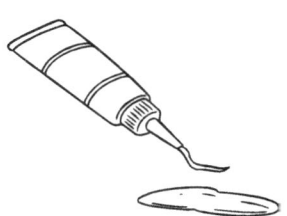

*"My heart is broken,*
*my mind, totally confused…*
*and my eyes feel glued shut,*
*sealed shut,*
*locked together…"*

You might feel very damaged right now… That's how I felt when finally, I got the right resources. I didn't know that understanding was a glue remover that would let me open my eyes. And once my eyes were open, I could finally see reality, make the right conscious choices, and heal.

I hope this book has the same effect for you. I hope it brings you enough…

**…Glue Remover**

# CHAPTER 1

# NAMING THE DAMAGE

Narcissistic abuse doesn't just break your heart... it rewires it.

It teaches you to doubt what you see, question what you feel, and apologize for breathing too loud.

It's a slow demolition of self:

- Your confidence is stripped and replaced with self-doubt.
- Your joy gets rewired into anxiety.
- Your boundaries erode until "no" feels dangerous.
- Your memories turn blurry from gaslighting.
- Your trust—in yourself, in others, in love—is shattered.

In the LGBTQ+ community, the damage can be amplified.

We come into relationships already carrying the scars of rejection, discrimination, and survival. A PS knows how to weaponize that history, twisting pride into shame, openness into vulnerability, and chosen family into collateral.

For people reading this book without understanding what narcissistic abuse feels like, what this type of person causes in our life, these are the names:

- Depression
- Sexual Trauma
- Financial Control
- Isolation
- Anxiety Disorders

This is what **they** leave behind:

- A brilliant human, questioning their worth.
- A voice that hesitates before speaking.
- A heart that flinches at kindness.
- But also, real love, support, honesty, light…

**You.**

And this is why this book exists: to name the damage, rip the mask off the abuser, and help you take back every stolen piece of yourself.

There's a version of you beyond the wreckage, one who loves fiercely, trusts wisely, and walks back into queer spaces without armor.

**The Sparkle will always be yours.**

# CHAPTER 2

# HIDE IT!

*"Cursed by the words you say. Owner of the ones you keep."*

You already know that narcissists flip the script **constantly**, but maybe you don't know the full dimensions of their game... yet.

The first thing I need you to understand and remember is: All the information you provide is going to be used against you, or to create a better plan to manipulate you, so be careful with:

**Books/Journals/YouTube:** If PS finds this book, they'll have a roadmap of their own personality and strategies, so PS will develop better ways to manipulate you, hurt you, and ultimately gain control (one more time). If PS finds your journal, they'll have a roadmap of your thoughts. If they can see what YouTube channels you are subscribed to, or your history, they'll know what resources you are trying to find. We don't want that! Hide all their possible resources.

**Talking for relief:** Be very careful with what information you share and with whom. This can feel isolating, but unfortunately, we are dealing with a very intelligent and manipulative person. They know when to cry, when to beg, and what to do in order to get information. Even if you can trust someone, that doesn't mean that person can't be manipulated. It happened even with members of my own family who saw multiple examples of abuse during my relationship. Do not blame them… If you have been manipulated for a long time, while witnessing their "other side," imagine someone who hasn't directly seen that or lived with it. If that happens, they will be just one more victim of manipulation on the list. Some good options for confiding are: people who are not mutual friends, your therapist, people who have already banned PS… Choose carefully, please.

**Reactions:** Narcissists LOVE provoking, poking, stabbing, in order to get a reaction from you. This is VERY important: Normally you react with your truth, and you may even think that you said what they deserved or something that will make them understand that their behavior is not good for you. And that is their goal! This is what we normally miss in the equation: They are not provoking you innocently or by mistake; they are looking for your reaction to TEST and gather information. So,

## Hold your unicorns, baby.

**If you react:** It means they still matter to you. It's a test, a win for them. Whatever information your reaction contains is kind of secondary (they'll use it though). That's why reacting in a way that is "punishing" them is not a good strategy, because you are still reacting and that's the goal.

**If you don't react:** This part is tricky. PS can see this as they don't matter for you anymore or enough. The best thing that can happen is: After many No-reactions, they won't get their supply (seeing you mad because they still matter) and they will discard you. (Congratulations! That's like winning a lottery even though maybe it doesn't feel like that, YET). The worst things that can happen are:

- The lack of reaction is used as justification to keep doing whatever thing they have done (knowing that it would hurt you), so they create a new dynamic because "as you didn't say anything, I thought it was okay." Now they have put the blame on you.

- "Next time it will be worse." If you didn't react the last time, they try to find a way to make you react the next time. So, be prepared because unfortunately,, with PS the war is never over. Until one day, **it is.** And that day is coming.

**The Honest Speech:** How many times have you sat down in front of PS and shared your feelings? How many times have you thought about the most effective way to make him understand your feelings? The most likely outcome is that they will immediately gaslight you, make you feel guilty, blame you, and so on. In some cases, it seems like they understand, and are really sorry... But we are not fools; we already know that it will happen again, they'll just create a more effective strategy. More discreet, with better lies, or maybe more destructive.

**I wish you wouldn't...:** *Hon, I wish you wouldn't have sex with... (name) because... (reason)...* Unfortunately, your honesty is going to be used against you. I could name a thousand examples of "I wish you wouldn't," and probably you can too. These are perfect weapons to use against you when PS needs supply...

**Messages through people (formerly called *Flying Monkeys*):** They know very well how to handle every single one of the people around them... and you. They know not only who among your friends or family members will *spread the message,* in order to hurt you, isolate you, or socially distort your reputation, but also which of your loved ones can touch your heart and convince you of something.

They will use this to either get a message to you, damage your image (and clean theirs), or win you back. It's time to activate a big filter. You can catch it in the air once you know *the dance.* What about if we call them… *Flying Monkeys?*

**DON'T CALL THEM A NARCISSIST:** If you do, they can find the same resources you are using to get out. They will learn them too, get sophisticated, and confuse you even more. Calling them narcissists is actually a gift to them.

…And sweetie, do they deserve our gifts?

*Okay… What should I do then!!?*

The only possible way out is going to *"zero contact."* That will happen over time, once you are ready. It is possible that right now that idea makes you shake, but don't worry. Soon you will be ready, and believe me, that day will be one of the best days of your life, even though you might not realize that until some time after it happens. If you are reading this, it is because inside of you, there's a message coming out, getting stronger and stronger every day (probably since a long time ago): *"DARLING, GET THE FUCK OUT! Either you leave, or this will end very badly."*

At this point, your goal shouldn't be to keep trying to make them understand your feelings, but to gain strength.

It's time to stop engaging and participating in their dark games and to put the focus back on **you.**

The best thing you can do with PS is to limit, control, and even transform the information as much as you can. Internally, we are going to work together to disengage from their dynamic, even if you are still in the relationship or connected to PS, and working towards that is your BEST move.

Ignoring them is one of the worst punishments you can inflict, so watch out! That can trigger their rage and make them take action, so:

- If you feel like you still need time to leave, play it safe. Instead of reacting, learn to "react." Give them a version of reaction that provides them with something, and still don't make them feel ignored. (We'll talk more about "Fake Supply.")

- If you have left already, IGNORE THEM. Go to Zero Contact as soon as possible and ignore their provocations FOREVER. Over time, they'll feel powerless and bored of trying, and they will find another victim.

Ignoring them is going to be a key factor in the process of getting rid of PS and finally healing. At times, it will feel VERY difficult, and you will have to use your determination and strength to do it. Remember: *"Replying to that message is giving away your power"* and at times it will feel pleasant, but let's analyze that for a second. Is it because you still feel the need to punish them? Is it because you still feel pain and you want to give it back? Is it that you miss them? It could be a sign that healing is not over yet and that a little more work within yourself is needed. As you become more aware of the full dark, blurry, and often BIG picture you are living in, you will disengage from it, and ignoring them will become effortless and natural.

## ♕ ACTION STEPS

Deep down you know it's time to go... It doesn't need to happen immediately if you are not ready, as long as you set up a firm goal: **To get ready to go.** I recommend that you read this whole book and get as many resources as possible before taking that step, if you are still in the relationship.

If you have gone but you are still engaging with PS... Now you know it's time to stop! And that is your new goal, **going from Engaging to Ignoring.** Sometimes it happens that full Zero Contact is not possible, because of shared businesses, children, and other ties, and these will be used as an entryway to keep bringing their games into your life and to hurt you somehow. You need to get as close to zero contact as possible, and communicate only when strictly necessary.

Any of these goals will keep you moving in the right direction. Which one of them is the right one for you?

.................................................................................................

I want you to answer these questions that will help you to bring back the focus to yourself:

Does it make sense to share/explain my feelings with somebody who uses them against me?

.................................................................................................

If I'm getting ready to go or if I have already left, does it make sense to still suffer/engage with their games?

.................................................................................................

Let these questions sink in for a bit. Take a breath... or a few.

Now, the last Action Step for today:

I know sometimes journaling (or visualizing) can feel kind of wishy-washy, especially if you've been stuck in survival mode. But stay with me, darling.

This isn't about rehashing your past or drowning in feelings. This is about your *future*.

And I know, when you've been stuck in something painful, it's hard to imagine freedom. It's hard to picture yourself fully you, joyful, safe, whole. But just *trying* is powerful. Just *starting* creates a shift.

You're about to send a signal to your nervous system that something new is possible. So let's go!

## Self Hypnosis 1

www.thesparkletrap.com/hyp1

What does your perfect day without PS look like? Get specific, describe how you wake up being free, what clothes you are wearing, what fun activity you would do ..Keep going!

..................................................................................................................

..................................................................................................................

..................................................................................................................

..................................................................................................................

..................................................................................................................

..................................................................................................................

..................................................................................................................

..................................................................................................................

(If you need more room to write, that's actually an excellent sign!)

## 🎯 KEY TAKEAWAYS

☆ All information you provide to a PS can and will be used against you.

☆ Be cautious about what you share and with whom, as a manipulator can use others to gather information or spread messages.

☆ Reacting to a PS's provocations is a "win" for them because it signals they still matter to you.

☆ The only way out is "zero contact," a process that happens over time when you are ready.

☆ Your goal should be to stop engaging in their games and focus on gaining strength for yourself.

# CHAPTER 3

# WASHING OFF THEIR MAKEUP

*"A narcissist…*
*is someone who wants, but doesn't provide.*
*is the one who will jerk off while you cry,*
*instead of looking for you and hugging you to comfort you.*
*is that one who chooses not texting you or replying to your message,*
*simply because it would make you feel good…*
*Is the one who will give you a home not to help you, but to own you.*
*At least a percentage of you.*
*And way, way, way*
*WAY*
*beyond…"*

Narcissists are **deeply insecure people** who, over time, have built a massive ego in order to cover their wounds.

They are constantly trying to gain security and hide their flaws **at all costs** by presenting themselves as **a victim or a hero.**

*Wait, what? Insecure?* YES, DARLING.

Despite what they constantly show the world, narcissists might have come from a difficult childhood. No one is born with a desire to control, manipulate, or cominate. But many are born into environments that teach them those behaviors are necessary to feel safe or significant.

In many cases, what we interpret as narcissism in adulthood may have its roots in early emotional injuries, moments when the child felt unseen, unloved, **or only conditionally accepted.**

- A child praised only for achievements may grow into an adult who depends on external validation.

- A child who had to suppress their needs to receive love may become an adult who manipulates situations to regain that sense of control.

- A child ignored or criticized for showing vulnerability may later arm themselves with charm, intellect, or superiority.

These adaptive behaviors are not conscious choices; they're often subconscious defenses, emotional contracts they unknowingly signed as children: *"I'll be perfect so I don't get **abandoned**,"* or *"If I never show weakness, they won't hurt me."*

These established beliefs can evolve during the life of a narcissist into very dark behaviors. But something remains:

**A deep fear of abandonment and rejection.**

That's why they won't easily let someone like you leave…

If you do, they will chase you and try to win you back. We'll learn how to protect from that once we are ready to leave.

It's pretty common that they will share in one of those *"honest-but-calculated"* moments, an emotional challenge, a childhood trauma they are still dealing with, an impossible relationship with a parent. And you are an empath, a sensitive person…

…so your brain says: *"HELP IS COMING THROUGH!!"*

A challenge has been created: to fix, to guide them through, to support…

**MISTAKE!**

At the same time, narcissists present an image of confidence, control, power that creates a sense of admiration.Again, your brain tells you: *"Oh! This person has struggles but still is confident… Someone to learn from!"*

**MISTAKE!**

…

**[You]** *Wait… What's happening? I feel something weird, but nice and sparkly around me…*

**Daniel:** *My love, it is The Trap. Here is exactly where it falls on you…*

*But it's nice! Why do you call it a trap?*

**Daniel:** *Darling, do you know those humane traps for mice?*

*It feels nice right now, because you are in it, smelling the cheese, but the door is not closed yet. And I don't like cheese, so let's replace it with a shiny, pink disco ball, okay? But very important, sweetie, by the time your empathy is peaking, you are already inside the trap. One more move, and the door snaps shut.*

*You will be alive, but under control and living in a limited space.*

*And if that space expands, it will be either because you escape…*

*Or just because you were given a bigger cage…*

*[to be continued]*

Most narcissists are VERY INTELLIGENT and they play their roles VERY NATURALLY. No doubt, they deserve an Oscar every year. This is something that took me a long time to understand: They stay three, four, or more moves ahead of you. They will provoke you, knowing how you will likely react, and knowing what to do afterwards.

But let's take a different approach…

Imagine David has a natural talent for the piano; he has been playing by ear since childhood. Rose wasn't born with that ease, but she studied for years at the conservatory. Who can compose a full symphony, with every instrument in harmony? Probably Rose.

What I mean by this is, yes, they are very intelligent and fog is their comfort zone, **but don't underestimate yourself. You are going to learn a lot with me.**

Let me give you a real case study, to understand how many times they craft plans to contain damages but still allow them to do what they want:

## Act I [Preparation]

[PS] *Hey I have bought us plane tickets to go to Portugal and I booked a great Airbnb…*

[Us] *Wow, that's wonderful! I'm so happy!*

## Act II, [The Slap on the face - A few days later]

[PS] *After our trip to Portugal I'm going to Bali with my ex for two weeks to celebrate my 40th birthday.*

## Act III, [Damage Control – Using the trip to France to counterbalance our reaction of "WTF!" To the trip to Bali (which, by the way, they also counted on]

[Us] *WTF?*

[PS] *Hey, but we have a great trip ahead, and by the way it wasn't cheap. Why don't we focus on that? Also, I'm giving you a great trip to Portugal, which I am paying for, and you want a trip to Bali too?? What's the matter, don't you trust me with my ex? I didn't realize how controlling you are…* [This is probably the moment when you shut the fuck up.]

## HOW MANY SLAPS?

It's hard to believe that someone can constantly live calculating damages, and improving ways to manipulate that are better adapted to you. And that's one of the ingredients of this deadly soup: We have good intentions, we are forgiving, and we need many (<u>many</u>) slaps on the face to finally realize that the person we love is actually cruel on purpose.

Narcissists are likely to perpetrate:

- Emotional Abuse (this is on a daily basis)
- Financial Abuse.
- Sexual Abuse
- Physical Abuse

Sometimes we need to look back with analytic eyes in order to realize that we are being "used" for their purposes. For that we need to ask ourselves the right questions, like:

- Do you file taxes with PS?

17

- Have you felt pressured to cross your boundaries with sex?

- Have you felt like "you are not enough" for PS?

- Have you been humiliated in front of other people by PS?

- Has PS shared with others exactly what you asked them to keep in secret?

If you answered yes to any of these, it is abuse and some of them might have been normalized in your head, in order to cope.


## GETTING INTO TYPES

So far what I have described could fit any narcissist, but here comes what blew my mind once I got the right resources:

### Overt and Covert

Based on my own experience and research, I found that one of the most visible signs to detect what type of narcissist you are dealing with is how they behave socially. Let's take a look:

**Overt:** This is the narcissism we can get more information about on YouTube or social media. With the right resources, you could "see it coming". It doesn't mean that you are immune to them! Remember, narcissists are very intelligent and great strategists.

They are normally loud in social contexts; they want the attention of the room. Either by shining or by destroying a plan, by being funny or by creating drama, it doesn't matter as long as they get attention, even if they need to degrade themselves or others.

This means that controlling you is not enough; they need massive social/sexual attention and validation.

**Covert:** Careful, careful, careful… This bull is wearing a costume. This type of narcissist is the most dangerous because it's very difficult to detect, very hard for us to understand what is happening, and finally find the right resources.

This type of narcissist plays more silent games, even though sometimes they can be loud too. If you are at a social event and you are getting noticed, or you are visibly happy, they will go on their phones while sitting in the shadows—they want you to think they are cruising on *Sniffies-HER-OkCupid*-Transdr—stay silent, ignore you, or cut you off with a humiliating "joke." They will try to fade your light, and if it happens that you are not feeling very well, for example, then they will shine, they will engage, laugh, make jokes. They appear to be reserved, or *"shy with fun exceptions"* but cruel AF, sweetie.

## THEIR BIGGEST FEAR

They make a big effort to present an image of perfection to the world, so what is the most triggering thing for a narcissist?

**Being exposed.**

Exposing a narcissist is NOT recommended unless it's used for your own protection. Focus all your energy on healing, not on revenge. More information in Chapter 14.

So, to summarize… (Straightforward, okay?)

**They don't care about you, but about what you give.**

That's it. Breathe it, darling. It's the raw truth.

They don't want you. They want **from** you.

That's why they make sure that you think:

*"Anything in their phone is more important than me."*

And that is only partially true. The phone is a tool to extract what they truly need: your reaction.

And while you provide supply, nothing will ever (never, ever) change, and the moment you cut supply… Bye-bye, sweetie… after big provocations, though.

## SO… WHAT'S "SUPPLY"?

Narcissistic supply is the emotional fuel that keeps them going. Praise, attention, admiration, envy, fear, even confusion…

**Anything that confirms their sense of importance, control, or superiority.**

They feed off the way others *see* them. And when the supply runs low—or worse, when you stop giving it, they panic, lash out, or discard. It's not about love. It's about keeping the mirror shining, no matter what it costs you.

In academic psychology, they'll tell you about *"primary"* and *"secondary"* narcissistic supply. Primary is the ego glitter: admiration, attention, applause. Secondary is the life support: loyalty, stability, even someone just existing to reflect their worth. Very cute, right?

But here's the thing: when you're in the battlefield, that language feels like reading a wine menu during a fire… I prefer to talk about **Noticeable** and **Expected** supply.

**Noticeable:** The one they can perceive directly from you. You being angry, your text messages feeling upset, the extra attention they get while they are silent… *"Are you okay?"*… your tears…

**Expected:** This one took me a really long time to understand, and I think it's the most important one. The expected supply is the damage they know they will generate without even seeing you. For example, all the hours feeling a pinch in your stomach, tracking, trying to understand, talking to friends about PS, going to therapy, hearing gossip from friends (that they spread) that causes pain… all the hours in *"Detective Mode ON"* (we'll talk about it later), all that energy and time… is also supply. And yes, they count on it.

**They expect it.**

That's why, when they know you are silently upset, and they call you, and you act totally natural and fine… they get angry. They'll generate a conflict somehow.

After condensing expected supply inside of you, they will expect a wave of noticeable supply after hours of silence while you were suffering.

Expected supply is also used as a way to control you: they know that while you are suffering, you are not enjoying yourself, and you are focused on them… Even if they never get to confirm that you were upset, they controlled that time of yours.

So when we start learning how to cut supply, the first one we will cut is the noticeable one. They'll keep poking (even harder) to get supply from you, and even if you don't react, while you feel anxious, insecure, angry, and so on, even if it's in silence, you are still their victim.

We will dive deep into this in future chapters.

# ♛ ACTION STEPS

Which type do you think is/was "your PS"?

.......................................................................................................

.......................................................................................................

What about supply? Can you recognize any past situations where you provided it? Write some notes...

.......................................................................................................

.......................................................................................................

.......................................................................................................

.......................................................................................................

.......................................................................................................

.......................................................................................................

.......................................................................................................

.......................................................................................................

Let's look back... Do you think you have ever been with a PS in your previous relationships? Let's make a list!

.......................................................................................................

.......................................................................................................

.......................................................................................................

.......................................................................................................

.......................................................................................................

........................................................................

........................................................................

........................................................................

........................................................................

........................................................................

........................................................................

........................................................................

........................................................................

........................................................................

........................................................................

........................................................................

........................................................................

[Just kidding...]

## 🎯 KEY TAKEAWAYS

★ A narcissist is a deeply insecure person who builds a massive ego to cover their wounds.

★ They may have come from a difficult childhood and developed adaptive behaviors to feel safe, such as seeking external validation or manipulating situations for control.

★ "Narcissists" are often very intelligent strategists who think several moves ahead.

★ They present a public image of confidence and charm, but will lie and manipulate for their own purposes.

★ You don't matter to them, but what you give them does.

# CHAPTER 4

# WHY ME, THOUGH?!

Because you are **irresistible** for a narcissist...

*BUT WHY, GURL?!*

I don't know you, but I know this: **You shine.** Maybe it's your charm, your humor, your status, or the way you light up a room without even trying.

**Whatever it is, they saw it, and they wanted it.**

You might be the cutest, super attractive, have a brilliant sense of humor, occupy a status position, or simply attract attention effortlessly, just because... somehow, you shine!

Why am I so confident to say this?

Narcissists **need** what is formally called *supply*, and they get it by *"dimming lights."* That supply is their interpretation of love.

If you were a wallflower with no spark, they wouldn't get the hit of dopamine they crave.

What excites them is controlling someone *shiny.* Someone who has power, light, charisma...

But there is still something missing in this equation, and it is key:

**You created this version of yourself, after struggles.**

Let's be real: just shining isn't enough to get hooked. What seals the deal is how your **subconscious was wired** long before they showed up.

Many of us had a hard childhood, maybe bullying at school, maybe a narcissistic parent... Our brain learned early on that *"we have to fight, beg, or prove ourselves in order to be loved and belong,"* and for us, that became *"familiar."*

You probably learned to survive in an environment where love felt like a roller coaster.

And because the brain fears change, it now mistakes chaos for love. Thank you, brain...

Over the years, you found your own place, your own sources of love, and you worked on yourself... Now, **after transforming yourself, you shine.**

Because of our environment (possibly other sources of healthy love), instead of becoming hateful people, we became sensitive and caring. We learned that we don't want people to feel like we once did.

So what are *our* core wounds?

### Abandonment and Rejection (Ding!)

Score! The same wounds narcissists suffered. It's just that they learned how to get love through manipulation and control, and you, through two different ingredients that are key:

### Empathy and Sensitivity

Without these two ingredients, the narcissistic cycle wouldn't be complete. They use these to manipulate you and bring you back after hurting you.

It's wild, two opposite systems originating with the same wound. And the tragic magic? Those opposite responses fit together like puzzle pieces. Dysfunctional ones. And our brain? It's detecting all this as familiar AF… like going back to our own childhood. That's why sometimes it feels so special, so magical, to meet… PS.

Even if "familiar" wasn't good, for your brain, the fact of going back to a well-known system feels great.

**Even spiritual.**

**But what about their empathy? Where is it? Or how does it work? Sometimes they seem to be empaths…**

- They can mimic empathy when it benefits them, whether it's to win you back, gain trust, or keep up appearances.

- They know what empathy looks like and when it will be most convincing.

- They learn what emotional responses get them what they want. It's not real empathy; it's calculated performance.

This **"weaponized empathy"** is part of what makes them so dangerous: they can seem **self-aware**, even **vulnerable**, just long enough to regain your trust before cycling back into abuse.

**Note:** Please don't be tempted to try to *"fix"* this person because you guys are connected by the same wounds… Not with love. Not with therapy. Not with enough chances. They won't change because **they're committed to power, not growth.**

Hey… Before you continue, just remember:

YOU SHINE

YOU ARE ENOUGH

YOU HAVE ALWAYS BEEN ENOUGH

AND YOU ALWAYS WILL BE

## ♛ ACTION STEPS

Let's create an empowering Glitter-chant, a spell, an anchor phrase, your personal "mantra." For example, *"I have myself and other meaningful connections; I am enough"*

.......................................................................................................

.......................................................................................................

.......................................................................................................

.......................................................................................................

.......................................................................................................

.......................................................................................................

## ◎ KEY TAKEAWAYS

★ You are irresistible to a narcissist because you "shine" with qualities like charm, humor, or charisma.

★ Narcissists need "supply," which they get by controlling someone shiny.

★ A key factor in getting hooked is that your brain has learned to associate a "roller coaster" of emotions with love, often due to a difficult childhood.

★ You and the narcissist share the same core wounds of "abandonment and rejection," but you respond with empathy and sensitivity, while they respond with manipulation and control.

★ A narcissist can "mimic" empathy to gain trust or win you back, but it is a "calculated performance" and not real.

# CHAPTER 5

# "WHO'S BORN A PIGLET, DIES A HOG"

While a recent study published in *The Journal of Nervous and Mental Disease* shows that narcissists can improve with long-term psychotherapy (two to five years), **many** other experts say: **narcissists don't change.**

This is one of those examples of *"trying to make the cat bark."* It won't work! Right? It's just a loss of your time and efforts. It doesn't matter if it's them going to therapy or your trying to make them understand their behavior. In this case, one of my favorite sayings from Spain applies perfectly:

**"Who's born a piglet, dies a hog." A narcissist won't change.**

We are deeply hooked on this type of relationship because of a key factor: **hope.** And I'm sorry if this sounds too straightforward, but what else do you need in order to lose it? Hopefully, the rest of this book will help you understand better and **focus your efforts on healing yourself.**

[You] *But sometimes it seems like they understand... and admit...*

[Me] *Sweetie, they'll deny it the next day... okay? Or they will be doing exactly the same thing next week...*

[You] *What if PS goes to therapy?*

## THEIR THERAPY... AGAINST YOU

Normally, narcissists will never admit they have *"something wrong,"* *"they are the problem,"* or *"they are the ones needing therapy,"* but believe me... If they see that as the only solution to hoover you back, **they will.**

And honestly... if that's where you are at in your relationship, that is not a good thing! This is going to be used against you.

As we said, they are talented actors, and they can **perfectly** confuse and lie to their therapist. They can flip the script so well that you may end up *"being the narcissist," "because their therapist told them so."* (Probably, that would never happen).

Therapy will only provide them with tools and resources **to manipulate you better,** and just the mere fact of going to therapy is going to be used against you. *"I'm showing you I want to change." "I'm doing my part." "I'm doing this for you"*...

Also, in my case, I was promised *"if you come back, I'm willing to go to therapy and become a better person."* I believed it...

**MISTAKE!**

After coming back, I would say, *"Are you looking for therapists?"* and PS would reply, *"No... Now we are doing better, we don't need that anymore."*

Do you know when going to therapy finally happened? When I was already gone, **for real.** And I would receive *"beautiful"* emails full of emotional bullshit like self-reflections and possible solutions *"provided by the therapist."* And you know what? I didn't believe anything at all...

**SCORE!**

There's something you need to learn: **Their only goal is to hook you back, NEVER to change.**

Now it is time to abandon hope (possibly you already have enough evidence to start working toward that) and start seeing that **there is hope for you.** A better, happier, and freer *you* awaits.

# ♛ ACTION STEPS

### Sweetie-Forms™

Sweetie… please, breathe and think about this:

Do you really understand that a narcissist won't change?

Yes? No? ............................. [please be a yes]

Do you understand that changing or fixing them is not your job? Plus, it's impossible…

Yes? No? ............................. [you got me shaking while you answer]

Do you understand that if therapy doesn't work, none of their promises will either? Sweetie, let's think about it…

Yes? No? ............................. […]

Please bookmark this page, or fold the corner, or put a clip, but keep it marked. When you are doubting, come back here and read your answers if they were *yes*. If there are any *no*, come back sometimes as you read and see if you answer differently… Maybe you should use a pencil…

## ◎ KEY TAKEAWAYS

★ Narcissists don't change, even if they go to therapy, and trying to make them understand is a waste of your time and effort.

★ The hope that they will change is a key factor that keeps people trapped in these relationships.

★ If a "PS" agrees to therapy, it is usually a tactic to hoover you back and will be used against you.

★ Their only goal is to hook you back, not to change or become a better person.

★ Focus your efforts on healing yourself because there is hope for a better, happier, and freer you.

# CHAPTER 6

# DETECTIVE MODE

*"It was just a weird text. Or a half-smile. Or a sentence that didn't land right. Just a little push... and... Welcome to Detective Mode."*

Our system has developed a mechanism, trying to escape from the cycle, that gets turned ON with the first breadcrumb you see, needing to **prove your own perception**. I call it *"Detective Mode."*

Here is when your intelligence starts to expand while you judge yourself for doing it, but we become **experts** on tracing breadcrumbs' meanings, detecting wishy-washy sharing (fog), tracking on apps ("Expanded Next Level Mode + IP Tracking"), reading micro-aggressions. Controllers? No... we have been forced to become an upgraded version of Sherlock Holmes.

The more we try to prove our perceptions, to not be treated as stupid, the more we risk crossing the lines of our own values. The more we learn new tools to investigate, the more we have to keep them secret, and the worse we feel about it... and all that feels like pressure. The pressure of judging yourself when somebody else has forced you to be there. With all that said, we become great detectives...

But let's think about how many hours you have been on Detective Mode in your relationship. **A lot?** Do you know what happens with all the time that you spent and you will spend in *"Detective Mode ON"*?

**They are the owners of it**

(Sweetie, can you rethink this, please?)

It's time that is lost in a trap laid by somebody else, time that you couldn't invest in yourself.

While you are trying to prove your gaslighted perception, **because they took you there on purpose**, they are observing your behaviors in Detective Mode, and you know what? That's it. That's enough to start receiving supply. The simple fact of your "needing more information" demonstrates to them that they matter. That you're not ON (Detective Mode)… but IN.

All that time is literally stolen from your life. With all those hours, you could've created four online businesses or written ten books. Or simply enjoyed your friends… but that pinch in the stomach doesn't let you do that. And to get rid of it, you need to KNOW.

All this is not only used as a source of supply, it is also used to manipulate the narrative, slowly, and label you socially as a reactive and controlling person. They will take the reactions from you that they're generating and use them against you.

To be even clearer, they are generating your **insecurity**, and then they are going to use it to their advantage. To keep their image as the strong and stable one, while you are seen as the unstable person.


## THE CONTROLLER

This is **key**.

Controller, reactive, intense, always jealous… unstable… triggered by your ex… **This is the classic first move** before a devaluation begins.

They need to put that label on you prior to starting the real damage. They will do this very early in the relationship. Normally, you won't even know about it, although you will detect *weird things…*

They need people to think that you are a controller. This will give them a wider range of freedom and the ability to control the narrative the moment you could expose them. Let me give you some examples of Classic Combos (you'll learn more about these very soon):

[Common friend] *Hey, you are cheating on your partner*

[PS] *Because I feel exploited! Daniel is so controlling that I'm just frustrated and angry…*

This is used as an SOS when somebody calls them out. If they previously labeled you as "controlling" when talking to that person, their story is going to seem pretty real. Even if they didn't like what they saw, now they know that it's better not to tell you anything. That person might be thinking, *"Serious stuff is going on, better not to get in the middle."*

This is VERY important for them.

They don't need too much to start, even if you are not yet in "Detective Mode On." They will even use something that they're agreeing to and even asking for themselves. BUT the game is to take you there.

**They want you searching for them.**

It's as simple as that.

**They want you insecure.**

**Any traces of your using the Detective Mode to prove your perception is going to be used to label you even faster!**

Please, my dear flamingo-shaped sweetie pie… we'll talk more about this but focus that time on yourself.

**Detective Mode is a leash.**
**Your nature is not controlling; they are trying to take you there.**
**Don't waste your freedom.**

# ♛ ACTION STEPS

Give me the list, honey. Don't be shy with me. I've been there, believe me... Which tools do you use in your *Detective Mode?*

..........................................................................................................

..........................................................................................................

..........................................................................................................

..........................................................................................................

..........................................................................................................

..........................................................................................................

What activities/experiences would bring you joy and take you away-ish from anxiety?

..........................................................................................................

..........................................................................................................

..........................................................................................................

..........................................................................................................

..........................................................................................................

..........................................................................................................

Do those bring you joy... or you want to do them because PS does them...? Sweetie...

Yes? No? ........................................

What can you replace? Something that is yours, darling. Something that brings you real joy, not "revenge."

....................................  ..................................................................................

....................................  ..................................................................................

.......................................................................................................................

.......................................................................................................................

.......................................................................................................................

.......................................................................................................................

.......................................................................................................................

.......................................................................................................................

.......................................................................................................................

.......................................................................................................................

## ◎ KEY TAKEAWAYS

★ Narcissists use small provocations—a "little push"—to activate your "Detective Mode," making you doubt your perception and try to prove them wrong.

★ The time and energy you spend in "Detective Mode™" is a form of supply for them, proving they still matter to you.

★ They use your reactions to manipulate the narrative and label you as "reactive," "controlling," or "unstable" to protect their own image.

★ This labeling is a "classic first move" before the devaluation phase begins.

★ Their ultimate goal is to make you insecure and keep you searching for them.

**Find me on the other side!**

www.thesparkletrap.com/qr2

# THE MEAT

*And suddenly, I was there… waiting for it. Fully aware it was coming. Like finally seeing the same damn structure, built with different tools. First, the moment of tenderness, support, understanding, connection… Then, there it is… **damage**.*

*And again that question:* **Why the fuck do I stay?**

This section dives into the structure of narcissistic abuse: how it works, why it repeats, and what it looks like inside queer relationships.

I consider this the heart of the book. Here, I offer you tools that changed my life: how to recognize the cycle, protect your power, break trauma bonds, and deal with *that* person.

Whether you're still in it, out of it, or unsure what the hell just happened, this section holds my knife block.

Use it to cut through the illusions.

Welcome to *The Meat*.

# CHAPTER 7

# SOCIAL ARMOR

And that day, when you see his rage and you face the disrespect, and you finally say it out loud, then someone looks at you and says, *"PS? No way. PS is the sweetest person..."*

Narcissists are strategic architects of social image, both their own and *yours*. One of the most powerful (and sneaky) tactics in narcissistic abuse is how they **manipulate the social narrative** to protect themselves and undermine you.

## THE FAKE *THEM*

They know exactly how to craft the perfect persona. Not just charming — *adored*. Not just liked—*admired*. They host, they help, they show up with gifts and generosity for people who barely know them. You see them volunteering to help a stranger with paperwork, offering a ride to someone they just met, organizing events, making people laugh, hosting like they're royalty.

Meanwhile, you're at home, exhausted, confused, or quietly breaking.

This isn't random. It's not because they're "just that nice." It's **insurance**. Social currency. A protective layer. Because if they ever cross the line with you, emotionally, sexually, financially, they've already made sure the audience is loyal to *them*.

## EARLY "CURATED GENEROSITY"

At the beginning, they'll often **go out of their way to be generous, helpful, or charming** with *your* friends, family, or even strangers they barely know.

They're building witnesses, pre-emptive credibility deposits in their emotional "bank account" with others.

> *"She helped me move for free, gave me legal advice, invited me to dinner... PS is great!"*

That's the trap. **The more people they charm, the less believable your story becomes.** They don't need everyone to love them. Just enough people to doubt you.

Suddenly, you're the "overdramatic one," the "jealous ex," the "one who can't move on."

They don't even need to lie about you directly. **The contrast between their shiny exterior and your quiet collapse is enough to cast doubt.**

And it hurts. Because you've watched them offer kindness to everyone *but you*. You've watched them treat others with the patience, warmth, and attention that you begged for. And deep down, a voice starts whispering, *"If they can be that kind... then maybe I was the problem."*

**No, darling! You weren't.**

That's not the truth. That's the spell. You were isolated while they built a fan club. You were shamed while they handed out praise. You were erased while they performed empathy in public.

- Their kindness to strangers was not love. It was strategy.

- Their reputation is not proof of your irrelevance but a weapon meant to silence your truth.

- You are not crazy for seeing two versions of the same person. You're finally seeing clearly.\

Let's start reclaiming the **clarity** that makes you stop questioning yourself.

## A NEW (AND OUT OF THE BLUE) FAKE YOU

Do you remember in the previous chapter I told you about "The Controller"?

Here's how they label you (and others) that way. And yes, there's **a lot** of psychological literature that supports this pattern:

### 1. Image Control for Later Denial

- If you ever speak up about manipulation or abuse, they've already "inoculated" others with a version of themselves that's so positive, *you* look like the unstable one.

- This is often called **"preemptive reputation management"** or **"credibility splitting."**

### 2. Private Devaluation vs. Public Praise

- In private: subtle digs, withholding, gaslighting.

- In public: they **praise you**, often *in exaggerated or perform-ative ways*, to make people think they adore you. This contrast confuses even you.

- It's part of keeping the story one-sided: "Look how well I speak of them; I can't possibly be the problem."

### 3. Triangulation via Image

- They may **subtly compare you to others** in their social circle ("*My ex never complained like that*," "*You should be more like X, X is sooo chill*"), using social comparisons to destabilize your self-worth.

- Or they'll tell others that *you're* the difficult one, so those people treat you with suspicion or pity.

### 4. Victim Narrative after the Break

- Once you break contact or expose any truth, they'll often **spin a victim story**: "They had trauma. I tried to help them. They were paranoid... controlling... unstable."

- Your emotional reactions, taken out of context, become part of the new narrative.

- **Their goal:** *Discredit your version of events before you even speak.*

### 5. Hijacking Your Community

- If they made friends with your friends, they might **stay in contact**, invite them places, or casually drop your name with subtle tension... trying to isolate you socially while pretending they "care."

### 6. Character Assassination

This is the broad term: deliberately spreading false, exaggerated, or misleading information to damage your reputation. It's one of the most common narcissistic tactics after or even **during the** relationship, and it often starts **before** the final discard so the smear campaign has momentum.

## 7. False Attribution / Fabricated Traits

This is more niche: making up entirely false "quirks" or "facts" about you — not just opinions. It's different from twisting something you said; it's *inventing* something that sounds petty, odd, or socially damaging.

- Examples like: "*He hates gay stuff*" (to frame you as self-hating in a queer context) or "*He doesn't like showers*" (to make you seem unhygienic) fit perfectly here. The goal is to create **sticky, image-based labels** that people will remember easily and repeat.

## 8. Preemptive Framing

They plant these false ideas so that if you later defend yourself or call out abuse, people already see you through a distorted lens. *"Oh, that's just Daniel being dramatic, remember how he's weird about…?"*

## 9. Humiliation-as-Humor

Especially in social/queer spaces, they often frame the smear as "a joke" so it flies under the radar. It becomes "playful teasing" to outsiders, but to you, it's a constant public undermining.

And that's how, one day, you become
*"the controlling, restrictive force that doesn't like showers
and hates-gay-stuff type of person."*
Or any other variation…
*Combo!*

But now we are building a voice.
Get ready, baby…

# ♕ ACTION STEPS

Think about the people in your life who were mutual friends with PS. For each person, ask yourself:

*"Do they make me feel safe? Do they respect my boundaries? Do I have to defend my truth around them?"*

The goal is to identify who in their life provides genuine support and who may be a potential "flying monkey" or a source of gossip.

Give yourself permission to limit contact with anyone who makes you feel unsafe or invalidated. This isn't about being angry; it's about building a protective, healing community.

#  KEY TAKEAWAYS

☆ Narcissistic abuse extends to your social life and public image. A key tactic is to manipulate the social narrative to protect the abuser and undermine you.

☆ Narcissists build a fake persona of being charming, generous, and adored to gain "social currency" and create a protective shield. They use this "curated generosity" to make people loyal to them, which makes your story less believable.

☆ They actively create a "new fake you" in the minds of others to discredit you. This involves preemptively labeling you with negative traits like "controlling" or "unstable" and using tactics like public praise contrasted with private devaluation.

☆ Their smear campaign often involves character assassination and false attribution. They deliberately spread false or misleading information to damage your reputation and create "sticky" labels that people will remember and repeat.

☆ The ultimate goal of social armor is to silence you and make others doubt your truth before you even have a chance to speak. You are not crazy for seeing two versions of the same person; you are simply seeing the reality of their calculated strategy.

# CHAPTER 8

# GLITTER, GHOST, SLAP, REPEAT

*"Once upon a time, a cute, clever, and wonderful frog was jumping around, looking for some water to refresh itself after a long walk. Suddenly, in front of its eyes, a shiny little pond of fresh water showed up! The frog didn't hesitate for a second and immediately jumped in.*

*It didn't realize it was actually a pot full of cold, fresh water... If the water had been hot, it would've jumped out very quickly. But that water was exactly what it needed, refreshing and nice. While the frog was enjoying a swim, the temperature started rising slowly, so slowly that the frog didn't realize until the water was so hot, that the poor frog was debilitated. Finally, it was rescued, taken care of, healed, and then... back to the shiny pot! Again, with fresh, cold water that will go to boiling soon. As time went by, the frog started to forget how its normal life had been and now became addicted to a toxic cycle of comfort, despair, and rescue that was hard to break free from."*

How does this look in real life? Let's dive deep into the drama...

**You gain security – They feel insecurity – They destroy your security – You feel insecure – They gain security – And back to the start...**

Narcissists use a cycle to keep you living in insecurity, to gain control, and very importantly, to keep you exactly where they want you to be. That cycle has four stages.

The structure of the cycle is:

**Love Bombing (Glitter) – Devaluation (Ghost) – Discard (Slap) – Hoovering (Repeat)**

## LOVE BOMBING

*"First impressions last"*

You have heard that before, right? It's key to understand this in order to know why we keep/kept coming back or stayed for too long.

When you meet someone new, especially if it's in an intense way (good or bad), a blueprint is created in your subconscious. An image, a memory, a special moment, or something representative for you during the beginning of the relationship is imprinted in your mind, and unfortunately (and many times subconsciously) you will go back to it many times.

This is something that holds the entire cycle as an image of "the good person" that you fell in love with, bringing you hope that "the good person" is somewhere there, waiting to come back.

But how do they create this strong impact? Through burying you in glitter, formally called "Love Bombing."

It's very common that, at the beginning of a relationship, we feel some kind of strong "soulmate connection," and then we fall in deeper while progressively bypassing red flags like a child going down a slide…

There are two things going on in parallel:

As we talked about before, most of us in the queer community have gone through a lot early on in our lives. In this phase, you will start noticing *small things* that your subconscious mind is starting to detect as a "familiar vibe," and is saying "finally!" It doesn't see it as something dangerous, but as your old natural environment, not good, **but familiar.**

In this phase, a narcissist will mimic your persona. They are playing with your empathy by presenting themselves as (**very**) similar to you and presenting similar wounds, core values, life experiences…

## Example 1: Same opinions or needs

[First date after Grindr meeting]

[Us] *Right now I'm not really into casual sex. Maybe if I had a relationship, I'd want to start close, and over time revisit that if we need to.*

[PS] *Wow… That's exactly how I feel too…*

Yeah, I totally get it…

*(+ PS's Classic Combos 3-4…)* [coming soon]

(+ manipulation combo) [coming soon]

## Example 2: Same wounds

[Us] *I had a difficult childhood… my mother… the school…*

[PS] *Ugh… For me, more than my mother it's my father… he's neurotic…*

There might be some truth in some of the hundreds of things they lie about, just enough to convince you… but in general, believe me, none of them are real.

What a turd, right? Couldn't our subconscious mind make us eat broccoli and date amazing people?! No, darling…

In addition to all this, they present themselves as generous people, helpers, carers, *"free spirits of Mother Nature"*… and we are *juicing…*

All this is the "Love Bombing" phase, glittering you until you almost cannot breathe…

**This is the image of them that we will remember.**

**The anchor**

[You] *What about Froggie…?*
[Me] *The frog is happy,*
*the water is fresh,*
*good food,*
*nails done,*
*feeling great in the pot…*
[Sounds of stove clicking — low fire is on]

…And here, in the middle of a chapter… I drop what some may find as a gem of help…

[go to page 235]
Please, DO NOT mention this section on social media.

## DEVALUATION

[Me] *...and slowly, very slowly...*
*the water's temperature started to rise...*
*very slowly, so slowly...*
*that Froggie didn't realize...*

As I start writing this section, a *"big anxiety breath"* floods my chest. This is a hard part to remember, and I have to say I'm **really** sorry that you are going or have gone through it, too... but, let's get some tools, okay? And the main one is to get **to understand** the techniques they use to "devalue" you, day by day, little by little, but eventually *in crescendo*.

In this phase, there is something essential for it to work: **the fact that you know.** So, either you see something by yourself, or they will make you see it by leaving **BREADCRUMBS:**

Think about it, sweetie. If you don't see, don't suspect, don't perceive, how can they hurt you? How can they distort your perception later on? How can they blame-shift to you? They want you to have *light evidence,* enough for you to notice but insufficient for you to have proof of the damage. They will make a suspicious comment, leave the phone "accidentally" unlocked with a conversation open (or an *app,* you know which one...), or do something as simple as not sending you that good night text you normally get. Anything that PS knows you will notice. And here is the next level: They already anticipate how you are going to react, what you will do next, and how they will devalue you again or hoover you back. Remember:

**They count on the damage and on your reactions.**

So, after you see something or crumbs are laid, there are different ways to devalue you and drain your security (so getting supply). You remember the *Combos!* right? Let's take a look at them separately so you become a pro in detecting manipulation. This will give you awareness about who you are with and strength in order to leave.

## MAIN TOOLS IN THE DEVALUATION PHASE:

Gaslighting has become very popular, so let's leave it for later. Let's start with things that worry me, being part of the queer community:

### Phoning

Yes, I have just invented that term, but phones are the very first tool of manipulation and devaluation for a narcissist!

With a phone, PS can:

- Micro-Discard you daily - you are trying to connect while they're on the phone, not even looking at you.

- Trigger not-enoughness - you are asking for more sex, just the two of you, while PS keeps using the apps all the time.

- Hide – *"I'm on a call"* or *"I'm taking care of something."*

- ............................ ...

The possibilities are endless.

### Triangulation

Let's start with the classic version of it because it's always there, and from there we'll make it more queer...

Triangulation is basically when they mention or bring in a third person with the intention of creating fear in you and the feeling of "needing to compete," or as they see it: **to make you compete for them.**

*They mention an ex, a friend, or even a stranger to make you jealous or insecure. Maybe they have an "important person" in their life (sometimes this is just another victim, suffering as much as you) and it seems like you have to share the time with your partner.*

- You're suddenly in **competition** with someone, real or imaginary.

- Goal: Undermine your self-worth and make you fight for their approval.

- These two points remain the same in the queer exploration of triangulation.

**When "Open" Becomes a Weapon:**

In healthy queer relationships, open dynamics can be, for some couples, empowering, freeing, and deeply consensual. But in the hands of a narcissistic abuser, "openness" becomes something else entirely: a tool for control, chaos, and power.

Here's how it plays out:

They bring in **a third**, with or without your consent, not with emotional clarity but with just enough ambiguity to leave you questioning everything. Sometimes it's an ex they're "still close to" or a fuck buddy. Sometimes it's someone "they just met and it meant nothing." Sometimes it's a friend who's "just very important" and maybe, somehow always around when you're not. Maybe all that at the same time…

You're told not to be jealous. You're told this is what freedom looks like. But your gut says something else. And that feeling? That twisting, heavy, hot/cold confusion in your chest?

That's triangulation.

They talk about how good the sex used to be with someone else. They tell you stories about how desirable they are to others. They flirt with others in front of you — but make you feel insecure for noticing. They post **just enough** on social media to trigger doubt. They tell you someone *"understands them better than you."*

It's not about love or connection.

It's about **getting a reaction** from you.

It's about seeing you compete, sweat, beg, or apologize. Why? As we said, **to test**, to measure, and if they see that triangulating keeps you engaged in suffering and insecurity. Then it never ends…

Those "others" are simply being used and weaponized. Sometimes narcissists can even get to engage those "others" in the battle and participate as real competitors, so that they get supply from different sides.

Now think about this: You try to find support and all you can say is "PS fucks with others" or "I got angry because PS had sex with..........." The most frequent reply you will find is "Don't you guys have an open relationship?" And you either desist, or you find yourself needing to explain and justify your feelings and perception.

In queer circles, where polyamory and openness are often celebrated, it can be hard to even **name** what's happening. You don't want to sound possessive or insecure. But here's the key difference:

**Ethical non-monogamy** is built on honesty, care, and equality. **Triangulation** is built on secrecy, power, and emotional manipulation.

When you're being triangulated, you're not in a triangle; you're in a **trap.** So remember:

- It's not "jealousy" if your boundaries are being stomped on.

- It's not "insecurity" if someone is intentionally trying to provoke you.

- If you're feeling constantly unsteady, confused, or like you're "losing your grip," you're not broken, you're being spun around in a game where you're never meant to win.

## Projection

This is exhausting too. When suddenly you are accused of something **they did!!??** Excuse me?? It even seems that they believe what they're saying!

Projection is the PS's twisted version of confession to avoid any kind of accountability and make you own it.

Instead of owning their behavior, they **fling it at you** like emotional glitter: shiny, distracting, and impossible to fully clean off. You end up apologizing for things you didn't do, doubting your own motives, and trying to solve problems that aren't even yours.

And in queer relationships, especially in emotionally intense, expressive dynamics, projection can come wrapped in progressive language, spiritual nonsense, or fake vulnerability.

Let's decode it.

### "You're so obsessed with appearances."

Translation: *I'm terrified of not being seen as hot, relevant, or desirable. But I'll accuse you of vanity first, so I don't have to face that.* Common from someone who body-shames you while constantly flexing on IG.

### "You're so emotionally manipulative."

Translation: *I guilt-trip, withhold, lie, and gaslight — but I've noticed you've started asserting your needs, so I'll label you toxic first.*

**"You're clearly not over your ex."**

Translation: *I'm not over mine. I compare us constantly and maybe even still talk to them. But I need to make your loyalty the problem.*

**"You need too much reassurance."**

Translation: *I disappear, flirt with others, invalidate your feelings, and now you're anxious. Instead of offering consistency, I'll shame your needs.*

**"You always want to be the center of attention."**

Translation: *I actually can't stand when the spotlight isn't on me — but I'll accuse you of it the second you shine.*

**"You're probably already cheating on me."**

Translation: *I'm thinking about it. Maybe even doing it. But I need to blur the lines and flip the script before you find out.*

**"You're the narcissist, not me!"**

Translation: *I've read enough pop psychology to weaponize it. If you start naming my behavior, I'll beat you to it, louder and with more drama.*

**Projection scrambles your reality.**

If you're sensitive, self-aware, or trauma-informed, it activates your reflex to *reflect*. And suddenly, you're in the rabbit hole of *"Maybe I am too intense. Maybe I do need too much. Maybe it is me..."*

But let me remind you: Self-awareness is not the same as self-blame.

**You didn't start this fire, you're just choking on the smoke.**

## Gaslighting

This is a whole dimension... Sometimes subtle and less frequent, mostly at the beginning; then it starts to grow in parallel to your confusion.

Gaslighting is a way to distort your perception of reality to make you question your memory, your emotions, and over time... your sanity.

It's not just lying. It's *strategic distortion,* dressed in "concern," "logic," or "love." It's a manipulation so slick, you'll end up apologizing for things that never happened.

Let's break it down:

**Classic Gaslighting Hits (Queer Edition)**

- **"That's not what I said."**
  Yes, it is. You remember it *word for word,* but now they say *you're twisting things.*
  Bonus track: *"You always overreact."*

- **"I never did that."**
  Except... you have receipts. Screenshots. A whole trauma museum. But somehow, you still feel unsure. Maybe you're being dramatic? Maybe it wasn't *that bad?*

- **"You're just sensitive."**
  This one comes with a rainbow bow. Often wrapped in *queer-coded language* like:
  *"You still have internalized trauma... that's why you're reacting this way."*
  Translation? *"You're broken. I'm enlightened. Let me reframe your truth for you."*

- **"Everyone else thinks you're unstable too."**
  This is gaslighting + triangulation — a two-for-one special! Now your truth isn't just "wrong," it's also socially invalid.

- **"WHAT ARE YOU SAYING? THAT NEVER HAPPENED!"**

In the meantime, we lose our nerve, and we... ENGAGE. The more this happens, the more we defend our truth. The frustration this can cause takes us to the limit, a limit that they will use to say things like: You see? Look at how you react, look at yourself, so angry...

You have to write this in stone inside of you:

**YOU DON'T NEED TO DEFEND YOUR TRUTH,
YOU DON'T NEED TO CLARIFY YOUR TRUTH,
YOU DON'T NEED TO FIGHT FOR YOUR TRUTH
TO BE ACCEPTED.**

This is, one more time, a way to make us engage in their sick dynamic, and they are not just avoiding accountability for their actions, they are also **TESTING** you.

Ultimately, when your own reality starts to feel unreliable...

You rely on theirs.

Forget about "trying to be fair" with somebody who plays in a different league.

## The Silent Treatment (Emotional Withdrawal)

Have you ever "won" and then you faced a cold wall for the rest of the day? Or maybe they are gone and they won't answer your messages or calls?

This can happen randomly, as one of so many ways to get supply, but in my case, I found that this was very often used as *revenge*. After pointing out something that was hurtful, after them feeling exposed, or simply because you are having a good day or good news in your life, this is a simple, yet effective, way to put you down, without even doing or saying anything. And that's the game. To ignore you on purpose. To make you feel that you are a piece of shit.

And how do we react? Begging, asking, trying to do something they like, making more efforts. And can you guess what they get…? *Supply!* (You are getting it…) This behavior is key to triggering your abandonment wounds, making you crave connection and either beg or apologize for something you didn't do.

Again, they are creating this nonsense, so limiting your engagement is key. They will get bored soon if you don't provide the attention they need, so be ready, because many times they will switch into a different technique that might work better in order to get what they want.

Anyhow, **limit your engagement or play clever.** Remember that this is not forever. You are dealing with it until you are ready to go or ban this "being."

## YOU ARE ENOUGH
## YOU ARE ENOUGH
## YOU ARE ENOUGH

### Hot & Cold Behavior (Intermittent Reinforcement)

I was talking to a friend who suspects that her mother may be a PS and she was sharing how yesterday, her mother was screaming on the phone *"GET A JOB!"* And today she suddenly sent her a text saying *"I'm so proud of my daughter."* She said that normally her mom is very rude, but pretty often, suddenly she writes her a text "full of love"… This is an example of *Intermittent Reinforcement.* Let's talk about how it sounds in a queer version.

They attack you and then, label you as reactive, too sensitive, jealous, you name it, and then, unexpectedly one day they look at you and say *"You're the most amazing person ever."*

This is a psychological tactic that creates emotional addiction through unpredictable validation. This connects you to the love bombing phase, when you could feel the *"high"* of being loved.

We need to focus back to ourselves, and dive deep into *"I'm enough."*

**Note:** Intermittent reinforcement behaviors are key to keep us in the loop. The entire relationship is based on patterns of intermittent reinforcement.

## Emotional Minimization

*"I spent the night with my fuck-buddies, but nothing sexual."*
*"You're overreacting." "It's not a big deal." "Stop being dramatic."*
*"You actually would have loved it… it was great."*

This is designed to **invalidate your emotions** so you suppress them or feel ashamed. The goal is to make you **question the legitimacy** of your needs and boundaries.

Either joking or being serious, they'll find a way to minimize everything that goes against their plans, wants, and needs. Many times, it's used at the same time as they gaslight you or are using triangulation, etc. *Combo!*

Our first reaction is to defend our feelings and boundaries, and I want you to think about this: Have you ever needed to defend such things in your life? Do you need to defend your feelings and boundaries with good friends and people who love you? It shouldn't be necessary, right?

## Blame-Shifting

*They explode in anger but say it's your fault for "pushing them."*

No matter what happens, it somehow becomes **your responsibility**. The goal? To **avoid accountability** and keep you in a guilt-loop.

*The Olympic sport of never being responsible.*

Blame-shifting is what PS does **when caught, cornered, or simply questioned**. It's the instant reflex to flip the script, redirect the spotlight, and leave you wondering if you're the one who messed up.

Let's say you bring something up, a boundary, a hurt, a concern, and somehow, within seconds, the conversation isn't about what they did… it's about what *you* didn't do.

Sound familiar?

*"You're always making drama."*
*"Maybe if you weren't so insecure, this wouldn't happen."*
*"You're overreacting."*
*"If you were fulfilling my needs, I wouldn't have to look elsewhere…"*

In a queer context, this can get even trickier. PS might frame your queerness, identity, or trauma as "the problem:"

*"You're projecting your internalized homophobia onto me."*
*"This is your childhood abandonment issue, not me."*
*"I can't be responsible for how your past affects you."*

Suddenly, you're not just hurt, you're also guilty. And confused. And apologizing.

[You] *But wait, is that gaslighting?*

Blame-shifting and gaslighting are close cousins, but they're not the same.

- Blame-shifting is about deflecting responsibility. The goal is to avoid being held accountable by pinning the blame back on you.

- Gaslighting is about warping your reality, making you doubt your memory, emotions, or perception of events.

| You say | They do |
|---|---|
| "That really hurt me" | → Blame-shift: "You're too sensitive." |
| "That never happened" | → Gaslight: "Of course it did. You're remembering it wrong." |
| "You said you were coming home" | → Both: "You never asked me to" (blame) |
| | + "You're making that up" (gaslight) |

If you're an emotionally aware, kind, growth-oriented human (a.k.a. many queer folks who've done some inner work), you're *already* used to asking:

"Could I have done something differently?"

And that's beautiful. Accountability is hot. Growth is powerful.

But PS abuses that part of you — using your introspection as a weapon to dodge their own.

## Controlling Your Access to Resources

*"I'm just trying to help"... said the spider to the fly.*

One of the more covert, but deeply damaging tactics PS uses is **controlling your access to resources.**

It's not always chains and cages. Often, it looks like "support." Like love. Like protection.

But underneath, the real goal is the same: **keep you dependent, keep you isolated, and keep you small.**

### Financial Control (Yes, Even If You're Not Married)

- *"Don't take that job, it's too far."* (And now you're stuck at home, isolated and under-stimulated.)

- *"I'll handle the rent. Just send me your half when you can."* (And suddenly your name isn't on the lease.)

Does it sound familiar to you?

In queer dynamics, where finances and roles can be fluid, this kind of control can hide in plain sight, behind ideas like "chosen family," "ride or die," or "let's build a future together."

But watch closely: if you start **losing access to your own autonomy**, that's not love, it's control.

### Emotional Resources: Rewriting Your Schedule, Your Focus, Your Life

This one's subtle.

*"Why are you seeing your therapist again this week?"*
*"You don't need that queer group, you've got me."*
*"Your friends are so dramatic. I just want peace."*

Little by little, PS rearranges your world. They insert themselves at the center of everything: your time, your attention, your choices…

And one day, you look up and realize: **You're orbiting them.**

Not your career. Not your friends. Not your truth.
Them.

### Social Isolation (But Make It Stylish)

This isn't always "You can't see your friends." PS might be more sophisticated:

- *"I just don't vibe with your crew. They don't get us."*

- *"She's clearly into you. I don't like how she looks at you."*

- *"You're not like them. You're better."*

- *"I don't like you when you're with..." or "You flirted with X, so now I'm too embarrassed to hang out with them anymore." Or they just make you feel really shitty if you want to see friends and they don't want to go, so you end up staying home.*

Translation? **Divide and conquer.**

They slowly cut your safety net, not by force, but by **shaping your perception** of the people who protect you.

They want to be the only one you trust. Because if they're your only lifeline, where are you gonna go?

What They Want:

Control.

Silence.

Power.

**Dependency = safety for them.**

Because the more independent you are, the easier it is for you to leave.

So every restriction, every "concern," every passive-aggressive comment about your job, your friends, your finances, is a step toward **disconnecting you from your power.**

## Comparing You to Others

*"Why can't you be more like them?"*

Yeah… that line should come with a hazard warning.

Once upon a time, you were the center of PS's glittery little world. The most brilliant. The most beautiful. The most *them-worthy.* But now? You're being casually (or not so casually) compared to someone else, and the message is clear: *You're no longer enough.*

Welcome to **Triangulation's sneaky cousin.**

*What's the difference?*

**Triangulation** usually adds a third person into the dynamic to create jealousy, rivalry, or confusion.
Think:

*"I ran into Ashley last night. We talked for hours… she just gets me."*

**Comparison**, on the other hand, might not involve direct interaction — but it still weaponizes another person's existence.

Think:

*"Kevin's so emotionally stable. I don't know why you're always so dramatic."*

Both tactics share the same goal: **To destabilize your self-worth and make you work harder to be "chosen" again.** It's psychological whiplash. You were once idolized and now you're being "motivated" through subtle humiliation.

- **It's not a compliment.**
  When they say "you could learn something from him," they don't want your growth — they want your submission.

- **It's not objective feedback.**
  It's curated. Strategic. They pick the qualities that hurt you the most to highlight in someone else.

- **It's not even about the other person.**
  It's about controlling you — pushing your buttons, making you feel replaceable, keeping you hooked.

In queer spaces, where community is sacred and often small, comparison can be especially painful:

- *"His drag is so much more polished than yours."*
- *"She's a real activist, you just post quotes."*
- *"You should see how [insert name] treats his partner."*

Not only are you being compared; it's often to people you know, follow, or even admire.

PS counts on this closeness to make the sting deeper.

**You don't need to be like them. You just need to remember who *you* are, and what you bring to the table, glitter, scars, and all.**

## Passive-Aggressive Comments

*"Fine. Whatever."*

*"If that's what you want…"*

These aren't neutral phrases; they're emotional booby traps.

Passive-aggressive comments are a way to express anger or control without direct confrontation. Instead of being honest, they punish you through guilt, sarcasm, or emotional withdrawal, leaving you confused, anxious, and second-guessing yourself.

In queer relationships, where emotional nuance is often celebrated, this can feel even more manipulative. The tone says more than the words, and the silence after? That's the real punishment.

You might cancel plans, change outfits, or apologize, all without them ever saying "don't." That's the goal: keep you adjusting, without taking any accountability.

**Bottom line:** if you constantly feel like you did something wrong but can't name what — that's not love. That's control wrapped in fake politeness.

To summarize this whole mess we call "Devaluation"…

**Lies, lies, and more lies.**

Narcissists don't just lie; they lie **strategically**. And worse: They lie **beautifully**. Just enough truth to make it sound legit. Just enough drama to make you question yourself. Just enough softness to keep you hooked.

They'll swear on their childhood dog's grave. They'll cry. They'll look you in the eye.

And you'll want to believe them, not because you're naïve, but because you're loyal, hopeful… human.

Sometimes they lie to cover betrayal. Sometimes they lie just to keep control. And sometimes, they lie for the thrill, to watch you spin.

Even when you *know* they're lying, they're so good at flipping the script that you end up doubting your intuition.

*"Maybe I misunderstood."*
*"Maybe I overreacted."*

No, sweetheart, **you didn't.**

Narcissists lie so much, they start believing their own versions. They rewrite history in real time. They deny what they just said. And if you catch them? They'll either gaslight you, guilt-trip you, or, surprise! Make it your fault.

Remember:

- Honesty isn't only about words, it's about consistency in actions too.

- Lies are the glue of the devaluation phase.

- If you feel dizzy, it's because the truth keeps shifting under your feet.

- You don't need to win an argument.

- You don't need to prove they lied.

- You just need to trust that you *felt* it.

In the middle of this boiling emotional soup (where you're *Froggie*), your brain starts **normalizing** what should be red flags.

Things you'd never tolerate from a friend or a family member, you start tolerating from PS.

Why?

Because a toxic mix of **trauma bonding**, the desperate need to regain your "*place*" in their life, and the illusion that "*getting it right*" will finally bring you peace hijacks your nervous system.

It starts feeling like a mission, a challenge, a way to prove your worth, even though you're still "*in love*" with someone who's hurting you.

The good news? **That's not love.**

And we'll dive deeper into that very real confusion in Chapter 10.

Please remember, the tools we just studied are normally presented as *Combos!*

[You] *Froggie… It's swimming slower…*
[Me] *It's losing strength and probably its confidence too.*
*The water is now pretty hot…*
*Don't worry, darling…*
*Froggie survives at the end, okay?*
*But not yet.*

# ♛ ACTION STEPS

I know… it's not the end of the chapter, but all this is a lot! So let's stop for a little bit…

How many of these techniques can you easily recognize in PS if you look back in time?

.................................................................................................................................

.................................................................................................................................

.................................................................................................................................

.................................................................................................................................

.................................................................................................................................

Many times the feelings of being like an angry child, where you cry, scream, beg… are overwhelming. We get so raw in our emotions that our childhood wounds reappear, deeper than ever, many times without us even knowing. I want to gift you with a self-hypnosis audio. A powerful tool to protect yourself and your inner child called "upgrading the child." I really hope you enjoy it.

**Self Hypnosis 2**

www.thesparkletrap.com/hyp2

## DEVALUATION

*"Not all discards are final.*
*Some are performances designed to hurt.*
*Others are tests to see if you'll come crawling back."*

Sweetie... I want you sharp here, ok?

There are many subtle discards that you have already normalized, and those are actually abuse too...

This painful-to-write section will cover different types of discard, but first I want to set this section in the right context:

## THE QUEER SET UP

In our community, many times we connect to our community through our partner, so if a discard comes (or it might happen even if you leave), they don't just remove you from the relationship. They discard you from the group chat, the weekends, the chosen family you thought you had.

For us, being discarded isn't just romantic. It's social. It's political. It's being exiled from the group chat, the beach plans, the karaoke nights, the living-room brunches... (We'll talk more about this in Chapter 17.)

The impact on our image of the after-discard manipulation in a small community like ours can be huge. And to finish marking you as the restrictive force in their lives, they will discard you in a way that sends a clear social message:

**Separating from you is a liberation.**

[Also a classic move, especially if you are the one breaking up.]

And many queer survivors stay silent after discard because PS has already rewritten the narrative socially...

Now... take a deep breath... and let's dive deep into discard types and what they look like. I'm starting with the *Definitive Discard* because it's the best one! They just drop you...

*Supply Discards* are temporary drop-offs, fake goodbyes, or disappearing acts, not to leave you, but to train you. To **test your emotional leash.**

But we got this, darling...

## DEFINITIVE DISCARD

Yes... you gave them your heart. They threw it out like a used tissue.

The *Definitive Discard* can hit like a slap or sneak in like fog, sudden or slow, but always sharp. One moment, you're fighting to keep the connection alive, and the next, they're gone. Cold. Silent. Detached. Maybe even with someone new. Or at least pretending to be.

Normally, when they discard definitively, they do it in a way they know will hurt. Often, when they are the ones discarding (not you leaving), they use humiliation or replacement.

Here is the main thing I want you to remember, my sweetie pie of the universe:

**being alone is the upgrade.**

You were never meant to be loved. You were meant to be used. And when your light stops feeding their ego, you become irrelevant. That's the ugly truth behind the discard: it isn't about closure, it's about control. They don't say goodbye with honesty. They don't offer understanding. They leave with a show.

You may feel confused, and in pain, but a part of you knows **you're better off.**

Sometimes it's because you set a boundary. Sometimes it's because you started asking the right questions. And sometimes, it's simply because they found a new *shiny toy*. Whatever the reason, the discard is rarely clean. They'll rewrite the story, paint you as "crazy," "controlling," or "toxic," and charm the outside world with a fresh mask while you're still reeling.

You might even hear from mutual friends that *you* were the problem, all while they play victim in a new narrative where they were the sweet, generous, misunderstood angel. And the worst part? That pain you feel? It's not just heartbreak. It's withdrawal, from the trauma bond, from the intermittent love, from the fantasy they built and you believed in. (More information in Chapter 10.)

But listen closely, love. Being discarded doesn't mean you were unworthy. It means you stopped serving their performance. And guess what? That's not a loss. That's a liberation.

## SUPPLY DISCARDS

During the cycle, you will face multiple discards. They measure the impact and hit, knowing your reaction and counting on bringing you back. These are *Supply Discards*.

A Supply Discard can be subtle or really painful, so let's throw some light and see what they can look like:

- Hanging up the phone and disappearing for a while in a really emotional moment for you.

- Secretly organizing an orgy without your consent, with random people... at New Year's Eve... [knowing you'd freak out.]

- Going partying after a conflict, or even a breakup, to send the message *"This is how much I care."*

- Going on a trip with *buddies* and ignoring you.

- Not sending you *"that text."*

- A combination of many discards like this at the same time.

Endless possibilities, darling…

Some are micro-discards, sure. But others? Massive. The more dependent they think you are, and the less supply you provide, the bigger the discard gets.

After these discards, they feed from your reactions, your emotional state, your tears. These discards aren't about ending the relationship. They're about training your nervous system. To react. To stay. To believe that maybe next time, you'll be enough.

The underlying message they want to send your brain (with both types of discard) is:

**I don't care about you**

[You] *OMG, Froggie!*
[Me] *Now it's cooked… fried…*
*But wait…*
*what if it was reanimated, healed,*
*and then put back in the pot with cold and fresh water again…?*

**Welcome to the Hoovering Phase:**
**Froggie's "care" services.**

## HOOVERING

*"From lies, lies, lies to promises, promises, promises…
(that you should NEVER believe!!) "*

If you look back, you may notice that the end of the devaluation phase and the beginning of the discard phase might look blurry… Let's look at both of those phases like a unique scene. The pain grows, confusion grows, and suddenly… *Slap!* Silence, and lots of pain. But then, hope comes back… Ugh.

Named after the vacuum brand (yes, really), hoovering is what PS does when they sense you're about to move on, so hurt that you're thinking about leaving, or worse, you're doing okay without them. (Sometimes, hoovering can happen even after months or more!).

Your glow-up, your silence, your boundaries? They're like a dog whistle for their ego. Suddenly, they remember you exist. And not just exist, you were *"the one."* The misunderstood soulmate. The one they *"weren't ready for."* The one they *"fucked up with."*

Cue the apologies. The love songs. The random text at 2:13 AM saying, *"I just miss us."*

Let's be clear: This isn't love. It's strategy. They're not trying to fix what they broke; they're trying to see if they still have access. Can they get back into your heart, your mind, your bed? Can they stir the old feelings just enough to reopen the door?

Sometimes they hoover softly: a story reposted, a memory shared, a *"hey, thinking of you."* Sometimes they hoover hard: full love-bombing reboot. Flowers. DMs. Long-ass emails. Fake growth. *"I'm in therapy now."*

And sometimes, they hoover sideways, using mutual friends, family, even your social media comments to remind you that they still exist. Why? Because your attention is supply. And **your indifference is a threat.**

Here's the cruel twist: **They don't want you back to build something better; they want you back to prove they still can.** And the moment they feel in control again? The cycle begins all over. "Glitter, Ghost, Slap, Repeat…"

So if they come back, and chances are they will, don't take it as proof of love. Take it as proof that you're finally healing. Because healing creates distance. And distance turns you from puppet into a missing toy. And honey, nothing haunts PS like a toy they can't reach anymore.

## SPECIAL ATTENTION TO… PROMISES

In this phase, they need to win. It's not a desire, it's something that feels like a real need for them, something that can even get scary and compulsive.

If the reason why you're trying to walk away is X, Y, or Z, they will promise you those things, many times in a "medium to long term." Not so much immediately, so they gain time, because remember, the goal is just to prove to themselves that they still have power and control over you, not to build something better. They will swear and even change for a while. **For a while, sweetie.**

"And this is the moment, after completing the first cycle "successfully," when you are not enchanted by the pink disco ball inside the trap…

but the door is now closed."

**– Sound of trap closing –**

# ♛ ACTION STEPS

Now that we have understood (finally!) the full dynamic of this relationship, let's dive into an exercise to go deep into our "I'm enough" part. Also it will connect you with your future self, the free one, the one empowered more than ever.

This self-hypnosis audio is crafted with love, and from the experience of "yes, it is possible." I hope you enjoy it and it gives you strength to continue in this process.

**Self Hypnosis 3**

www.thesparkletrap.com/hyp3

## ⦿ KEY TAKEAWAYS

★ The narcissistic cycle of abuse consists of four phases: Love Bombing (Glitter), Devaluation (Ghost), Discard (Slap), and Hoovering (Repeat).

★ Love Bombing: This initial phase creates an intense "soulmate connection" that becomes a blueprint of "the good person" you remember, giving you hope throughout the rest of the cycle.

★ Devaluation: This phase involves techniques like Triangulation (creating jealousy or competition with a third person) and Projection (accusing you of their own behaviors) to erode your self-worth.

★ Discard: This phase is when the narcissist consciously ends the relationship, either temporarily or permanently, because you've stopped providing supply. In the queer community, this can also mean social and emotional exile from a chosen family.

★ Hoovering: After a discard, they will try to lure you back with apologies and promises, not because they love you, but to see if they still have access to their supply.

# CHAPTER 9

# SEX THAT HURTS... AND NOT IN A GOOD WAY!

We have talked about weaponizing "openness," but let's dive deeper into sex inside a toxic relationship with a PS. Unfortunately, the limits here just keep expanding, and the feelings of "not-enoughness" or even feeling like "the slut," and not just as a fun role, grow and grow...

When I got hooked into "the relationship," at the beginning, we were "open" but without sharing, "to not hurt each other." Then we started having "innocent threesomes," saying it was our first time having a threesome with our own partner. Then the slow boil took over, and it got **totally** out of control over time.

Let me be very firm around this: Sex is great, exploring is great, but having someone pushing your boundaries against your will is not great, **it can be abuse**. It doesn't matter if you are being pushed to have a sexual experience you don't want or to have sex with someone you don't want to have sex with, it can be abuse.

Narcissists are normally very sexual and good at the art of seduction. It's usually one of the main hooks and also one of the main reasons to suffer.

Think about this... for narcissists, seeing you have sex **the way they want** gives them a huge sense of power, control, and domination.

Seeing you doing something you don't want to do, even feeling bad, but still doing it *"for them"* is a turn-on. But get ready, because the fact that you did it will go against you too. Once you start complaining, they will say things like *"You actually liked it"* or *"I saw you having fun"*.

They kept track. If you said no today, tomorrow they'd be cold. If you didn't initiate, they'd say you're not attracted to them. If you enjoyed it, they'd use that moment to demand more. Intimacy becomes a debt you can never repay.

They are experts in locating their fantasies and sexual dreams **outside your boundaries.**

By using manipulation, they will make you feel bad for not *"fulfilling their sexual needs."* They will use previous sexual experiences to push you a bit more, and they will make you feel like you are not enough for them.

In queer spaces, sex can feel like currency. Like proving your value. Like proving you're not "too broken" or "too boring." But your worth isn't measured in how much you give, it's in how deeply you feel safe and good with yourself.

**Note:** Many of us come from a childhood where we felt different. When connecting was hard. Now we feel free, and part of a community, but our brain is still wired to crave connection. Have you felt lonely or empty after having sex? Have you ever felt lonely or empty while in a relationship with a PS? What we crave is **real connection**, and we have to be careful when trying to put bandages on bleeding wounds. Real connection comes from our inner healing, not from the amount of sex we can have.

## THIS IS NOT SEDUCTION. IT'S PSYCHOLOGICAL COERCION.

They mix shame, desire, guilt, and pressure, and suddenly, your 'yes' isn't coming from excitement, **it's coming from fear of abandonment,** rejection, or being compared to someone else. That's not consent. That's survival.

For many queer folks, it's easy to confuse "sexual freedom" with **sexual submission**, especially when wrapped in language like: *"I thought we were sex positive." "Don't be so vanilla." "You're just insecure."*

But sex positivity doesn't mean ignoring your discomfort.

**It means respecting boundaries, not bending them until they snap.**


## SHAME IN THE SHEETS

You might find yourself walking away from an experience and suddenly crying in the shower. Or needing to disassociate during sex. Or hearing your friends say, *"Wow, you're so open,"* while you're silently thinking, *"No... I'm just trying not to lose PS."*

No, it's not kink. It's the trauma loop.

And yes, they will use your *"openness"* against you. If one day you say no, suddenly you're: "boring," "old," "prudish," or "selfish."

**Narcissists love playing both roles:**

They want you to be wild, so they can degrade you.
They want you to be hesitant, so they can shame you.
So... is it about sex... or about power?


## THE SADISTIC EDGE OF NARCISSISTIC ABUSE

Not every narcissist is sadistic, but many exhibit **sadistic traits**, especially when they feel their control is slipping. It's **intentional harm**.

According to Shahida Arabi and other researchers, many narcissists show behaviors that **border on psychopathy:**

- Lack of empathy.
- Superficial charm.
- Exploitation.
- Sadism.
- Emotional manipulation for pleasure or gain.

But the real twist? Many of them **know** what they're doing.

They're smart enough to **perform empathy**. To cry on cue. To say all the right things. Not because they feel it, but because they know **what it would look like** if they did.

That's not clumsiness. That's **calculated cruelty**.


## WHAT SADISM CAN LOOK LIKE IN QUEER TOXIC RELATIONSHIPS

- *"I wanted to see how far you'd go for me."*

- *"I knew it would hurt you… that's why I said it."*

- *"You're crying? That's dramatic. I barely touched you."*

- *Telling others your secrets or mocking your vulnerabilities behind your back.*

Sadistic narcissists enjoy **watching you squirm**, beg, or break. Not because they're impulsive, but because **they want to feel powerful**.

This is the **darkest flavor** of PS. The one that punishes your joy. The one that pushes boundaries just to feel the high of your collapse.

And that's how my story ends… with me breaking and collapsing over and over again while asking, "why am I not enough?"

## EXCUSE ME... WHERE IS MY SEX?

Here it is, another *Classic Combo*. We go from talking about pushing your boundaries to... nothing.

Sex as discards.

Imagine waking up and touching the person next you (who woke up and is reading news on the phone). You start trying to initiate something fun... and you end up with PS touching your pickle while looking at the phone... and then just nothing. More phone.

Imagine feeling horny, getting naked, and putting your sexy body in front of your "beloved partner"... and seeing that PS keeps staring at the TV, and not even looking at you.

Ouch... But you know what? Fuck you, PS.

The feelings of "not-enoughness" start peaking...

But here's the thing: they don't want to fuck with you, but they don't want you to masturbate either... Is any of this sounding familiar, sweetie? I truly hope not...

Maybe they are open to threesomes, orgies... but alone with you...?

## THE SEX WAR GAME

You don't need to be in a narcissistic relationship to experience this, but with PS it can become like a war. You leave breadcrumbs for me to know that you're having sex, so I have sex. In case you have sex tomorrow, I'm going to have sex twice today, and maybe tomorrow, and as I'm angry, I'm going to also leave breadcrumbs for you to find and...

This is not sex for joy. This is supply going back and forth, while only one of you is really enjoying it…

This is feeling behind, needing validation, needing to feel sexy for someone…! But darling, it's not because you really, truly want it.

## SO, WHAT'S HEALTHY?

Let's flip the narrative for a second.

- Healthy sex is mutual.
- It's free of pressure.
- It respects boundaries, even if they change.
- You feel safe before, during, and after.
- You're allowed to say no without being punished emotionally.
- You have mutual agreements that are respected.

## WHAT TO DO?

Narcissists are experts at creating feelings of "emotional debt" in you. Many times, that is how they end up getting what they want, often, crossing the line of sexual abuse. That emotional debt you may feel is unreal. You don't owe them anything; they are manipulating you.

You don't have to do anything you don't want.

It's time to set up a firm boundary, sweetie pie. An indestructible one.

**Note:** If you are in danger, please get professional support as soon as possible.

**Please read carefully:**

## YOU ARE ENOUGH, YOU ARE ENOUGH AND MORE THAN ENOUGH

# ♛ ACTION STEPS

Ask yourself:

Have I ever done something sexual just to avoid conflict?

..........................................................................................................

..........................................................................................................

..........................................................................................................

..........................................................................................................

..........................................................................................................

Have I ever felt more disconnected after sex than before?

..........................................................................................................

..........................................................................................................

..........................................................................................................

..........................................................................................................

..........................................................................................................

Do I feel ashamed of my body or preferences after being with PS?

..........................................................................................................

..........................................................................................................

..........................................................................................................

..........................................................................................................

..........................................................................................................

Have I ever felt something alarming instead of protection by my partner while struggling before/during/after sex?

...................................................................................................................

....................................... .............................................................................

....................................... .............................................................................

........................................... .........................................................................

...................................................................................................................

Let's think of it... even if it hurts. Have you been through an experience (or more) of sexual abuse?

If the answer is yes... know that you're not alone. And that this chapter is NOT about blaming yourself, it's about reclaiming your body, your boundaries, and your sexuality.

Sweetie. If you can, it is time to stand up, and give yourself a hug... a long one. Close your eyes and touch your own arms, and say, *I got you, baby. Let's breathe a little bit*... (That's what I did, right after finishing the first draft of this chapter)

## 🎯 KEY TAKEAWAYS

✫ Sex with a narcissist is often about power, control, and domination, not mutual connection.

✫ They may use psychological coercion, mixing shame, guilt, and pressure to make you cross your sexual boundaries.

✫ For queer people in "open" relationships, this can be even more confusing, as the abuser may frame their behavior as "sexual freedom" while it is, in fact, control.

✫ After sex, you may feel lonely or empty because you are craving real connection, not a transactional experience.

✫ Some narcissists exhibit sadistic traits and enjoy watching you hurt, making the abuse intentional and calculated.

# CHAPTER 10

# T-BOND

*"Some Sparkles Hurt...*
*But every breakthrough, every 'aha moment',*
*is a thread loosened in the electrified web that seems to hold you.*
*But... You don't have to untangle the whole thing to escape.*
*You just need to make enough space to slip through the holes."*
　Ok... Let's tackle *"the elephant in the room"...*

**Why the Fuck Do I Stay?!**

*Breathe in, darling... hold it... and breathe out...*
*All the judgment over yourself...*
*Let it go*
*All the pressure from yourself and others...*
*Let it go, my love*
*You are not the one choosing to tolerate, to justify, to stay, to miss, to hope...*
***your wounds are,***
***your chemistry is.***
*Give yourself compassion,*
*it's okay, my love. .*

It's like a slow, yet powerful, momentum bringing you back...
We are like incandescent rocks floating on a river of sticky lava,
carrying us at its will. I call this feeling *"the pull."*

It feels as if something supernatural was keeping us connected to them, like an elastic where we are one at each end, and the harder we pull away from each other, the stronger the force bringing us back in the middle.

**And logic doesn't matter...**

So, after coming back from being devalued and suffering a cruel discard, pressure arises. You know that logically you have "tolerated" a huge red truck coming toward you at 200m/h. And you don't understand how or why you are doing it. You are just coming back and you start judging yourself... You know that was *too much*, and while you feel stupid and hopeful at the same time... you're hurt.

So, you call your sister-in-law, the one who always helps you, or that great friend, and you tell them what happened. You need support. And their best answer is:

**get the fuck out.**

But that just adds... **pressure.** So next time, you shut the fuck up, right? And you swallow it all alone...

## ABUSE THAT HIJACKS THE MEANING OF LOVE

Trauma bonding often echoes wounds from childhood, where love and pain came in the same package.

In trauma bonding, the pain becomes proof that the love is real, that you're fighting for something meaningful. The more it hurts, the more convinced you are that it matters. Because why else would you be here?

And then... The *"my sparkle will fix it"* fantasy...
"If I am loving enough they'll be fixed."
I think you know what my next word is...

## MISTAKE!

You learned to measure love by suffering. The more you hurt, the more it must mean. But that was never true. Love doesn't require you to bleed to prove it exists.

## WHEN DOES IT START?

Trauma bonding starts being built the first day you meet PS. During the first love-bombing phase, they are future-faking, and "showing" you the same wounds you suffer... And, as I said, first impressions last...

That image you have of PS is like an **anchor** in your subconscious. So during the devaluation phase and a discard, your mind is looking for the version of that person that you knew as real. And there it comes... **hope**. Nostalgia for the version of PS that you met. So when they start hoovering, showing that version again (to some degree), your heart melts... Your eyes juice, your brain juices, and other parts juice too...

Normally, the first full cycles are more intense, with perfectly crafted love-bombing and tons of future-faking, glamorous promises, and softer devaluation and discard phases. But the dynamics of *Intermittent Reinforcement* are already happening...

Love + Pain + Love + Pain + Love... [Could be eternal]

Security + Ambiguity + Security + Ambiguity + Ambiguity +...

And this is the recipe that makes hope stronger and stronger: Your brain starts learning, after the pain, something good is coming… That's why our dear *Froggie* comes back into the water.

It's like waiting for the prize in a gambling machine while you spend more and more money.

And no, it's not just emotional or narrative… it's dopamine, cortisol, oxytocin…

And like gambling… **it's addictive.**

Now think about when your friend told you *"Get the fuck out"*…

Would somebody tell an addicted person, *"Give me the drugs. Cured! You can go"*?

It doesn't work like that, right?

## DOES IT HAPPEN FOR PS TOO?

Do you remember the hoovering phase?

**They don't let you go.**

They're addicted too, but not to love. To power. They don't feel the pain of disconnection like you do, but the craving for control.

Their brains are also addicted, but with a big difference… they are the ones holding the knife and the bandages.

While they see you as a source of supply, they will keep trying to provoke you or to win your heart back in order to get it.

## THE CHEMICAL SETUP

This is the time to stop judging yourself, my love. I want you to see even more clearly how the cycle of chemicals going through your brain is keeping you stuck, and feeling guilty for not leaving, etc.

- They love-bomb you: dopamine hit.
- They devalue you: cortisol spike.
- They pull away: panic.
- They return with softness: relief.
- Repeat.

This cycle rewires your nervous system.
   As I said earlier…

it is **NOT** love,
it is withdrawal.


## WHEN QUEER LOVE BECOMES A LEASH

Maybe they talked "open relationship" like it was liberation, not erosion. Maybe they called you "free" while slowly dimming your shine.
   In queer spaces, where "openness" is trendy and "drama" is glamorized, abuse hides behind sparkle. You're not chasing them. You're chasing the version of them that never existed, except in the love-bombing phase. And the longer you stay, the more you'll wonder…

is this pain just part of the package?

   No, it's not.


## THE LOYALTY TO PAIN

This is the part that hits hardest. You weren't weak. You were loyal. You wanted to fix it, to earn it, to prove them wrong, to make them understand their own manipulation…

But love that constantly hurts isn't love. It's submission. Emotional servitude.

They taught you that staying was noble. That leaving meant you were selfish. That if you really cared, you'd hold on longer.

None of that is love. It's control.

## THE CRACK

Inside it starts, inside it ends... Breaking free from trauma bonding happens inside of you, and it can even happen (at some level) inside the relationship, before it actually ends.

That's the crack in your trauma bonding: awareness and self-empowerment.

Along the way in this book, you have found tools to stop engaging, control supply, detect the traps... All the time you don't invest in reacting to the cycle, you are thinking better. Now, you are imagining a new and better life for yourself, looking at your relationship from the outside and getting stronger and stronger every day.

You don't have to break the whole bond today. You just have to see it. That's how it starts. Each time you *don't* respond, *don't* justify, *don't* explain, the spell weakens.

In the next chapters, I'm going to give you more resources and ways to navigate all this, my sweetie. We got this, okay?

Please, don't miss the action steps today... I'm sure they will help you.

## GOLDEN HOOKS

Once we start thinking about leaving, something very common happens. It happens to all of us and it's something to look out for.

This is normally the strongest reason that keeps us coming back or simply not leaving.

Imagine that you decide to leave tomorrow. Think about it. Imagine going with your suitcases through the door. Do you feel a pinch in your stomach? Look at it. Why that pinch? Right now, your head is being flooded with reasons to stay:

- The dog
- The mortgage
- The visa
- Kids
- Your finances
- ..............................

Let me tell you something: All that is your T-Bond trying to hold on to something strong enough, to avoid facing the breakup, **not real hooks that make it worth it to stay.**

We need to locate all those Golden Hooks sabotaging you. Sometimes it's only one, a strong one. Sometimes it can be more than one. We need to be hyper-aware of these hooks and work in advance, because we know now they will sabotage our plans.

By the way… those Golden Hooks might be exactly the things you need to take care of before leaving.

**I said take care of, not use them as an excuse to stay living in abuse**

## FLIP THE ZERO CONTACT

Darling, have you thought about this? When we are hooked to PS we get kind of blind, but what is it exactly that we can't see?

**Ourselves**

Slowly, we move away from ourselves, **going zero contact with our own spirit**, and our entire vision is around them. It's time to flip that, right? We should have Zero Contact with them!!

Every day away from PS, choosing ourselves instead of answering that text, or checking our phones is a day flipping the zero. Every day we get a little bit more back from that 100% that was once ours. But time, awareness, support, and self-care speed up the process. We got this.

10% back feels better than 0.

Then 40%…

60%…

Every day without PS will feel better. You don't even need your 100% back in order to start building a great life!

## THE WEIRD SILENCE

I want to share something with you that helped me a lot. It's a simple sentence that gave me strength to keep going towards *not coming back…*

Trauma bonding feels many times like a weird silence, even when they are still there but you are more and more disconnected. But, especially once you go, your system is really wanting a text, a call, some noise… and many times we face nothing (which is actually good…). In those moments, the feelings of emptiness are heavy, and we want to fill the weird silence inside of us, but…

**in that silence is your new air**

That silence is where your new peace awaits. It feels weird because you are not used to having peace anymore, but there it is. In that silence, you have the necessary room, and bandwidth to start crafting a new and beautiful era.

## FINAL TRUTH BOMB

You didn't fall in love with them. You fell into a pattern designed to keep you spinning, small, and doubting your power.

But guess what? You're waking up. You're stronger than they ever expected. And this time… **love won't be a leash.**

You don't owe your loyalty to pain. You owe it to your future. And trust me… there's a version of you out there in the future, radiant, whole, and at peace, already thanking you.

# ♕ ACTION STEPS

**Notice your breath.** Is it shallow? Are your shoulders tense? Has your jaw been tight all day? These are signs your nervous system is cycling through trauma, not romance.

**Name it.** Say it out loud (away from PS!): "This is a trauma bond. I'm not in love, I'm in a cycle." Repeat it every time you feel "the pull."

**Feel the withdrawal.** If it hurts to leave, that's proof of the addiction, not proof you belong together. Any Golden Hooks popping up in your head?

..................................................................................................
..................................................................................................
..................................................................................................
..................................................................................................
..................................................................................................
..................................................................................................

**Reclaim the narrative.** Write down what they made you believe about love, safety, and your worth. Then rewrite it. Make a little ritual, burn it (safely please), bury it under a tree... (Don't let "*anybody*" see it.)

..................................................................................................
..................................................................................................
..................................................................................................
..................................................................................................
..................................................................................................

**Create a Detox Toolkit.** When you want to reach out, instead: call a friend, listen to a self-hypnosis audio, move your body, read this chapter again, take a shower, or scream into a pillow, whatever keeps you safe.

...................................... ...............................................................

............................................ ......................................................

............................................................................................................

............................................ ......................................................

...................................................... ........................................................

............................................................................................................

**Self-Hypnosis 4:** This is the most important piece of digital content in this book. Please don't underestimate it. Try to listen to it for 21 days, at least once a day. [Inside the next QR Code]

## ◎ KEY TAKEAWAYS

☆ Trauma bonding is the reason you stay, not because you are stupid, but because your wounds and brain chemistry have been hijacked.

☆ The cycle of "Love + Pain + Love + Pain" creates an addiction to the unpredictability, making your brain believe "after the pain, something good is coming."

☆ The trauma bond is an emotional addiction powered by dopamine and cortisol, and it feels like withdrawal, not love.

☆ You don't have to break the entire bond all at once; awareness and disengaging from the cycle is the first crack in the prison wall.

☆ The "weird silence" after leaving is not emptiness, but your new air.

**Find me on the other side! + Self-Hypnosis-4 [Important]**

www.thesparkletrap.com/qr4

# GETTING THE SUITCASE READY

[PS's future mind]

*When did it start?*

*When did you decide you were leaving?*

*When did it start?*

*The moment when I was still thinking I was hurting you, but you were gone inside…*

*How many moments was I thinking you were pissed, at home, waiting…*
*but you were…*
*…focused…*
*…preparing…*
*…**enjoying**…*

That's the question that we will **NEVER** answer. That's ours.

You don't owe honesty, loyalty, or truth to an abuser. Enough. Someone who manipulates, hurts and disrespects you on purpose doesn't deserve access to your truth.

Soon you'll look back and a smile will pop onto your face, the smile of:

*"I did it... I flipped it... and I won.*

*And you will never know what was actually happening.*

*While you were too confident thinking I was dependent, thinking I would come back like I always did,*

*I was...*

**...Getting the Suitcase Ready."**

# CHAPTER 11

# THE FLIP

*"And suddenly, you get to see it.*
*What actually connects the dots…*
*is never being able to connect the dots!*
*That's when you see it.*
*Manipulation…*
*Never Knowing and Never Winning.*
*The Never Connecting Dots.*
*That's the name of the game."*

[You] WTF Daniel?

*Yes, it is hard to understand…*

*But what specifically is hard to understand?*
*That sentence?*
*To finally see that you are actually playing connect the dots*
*and investing too much*
*time/effort/sanity?*
*Or the manipulation around you?*

*-…-*

*Let's breathe together, my love…*

There's a reason you're here with me now. A moment. A shift. A new event, a new discard, tells you, deep down: *"Enough"*.

In my case, the night of my birthday changed everything. I understood the hidden cruelty and the levels of manipulation and rage that a PS can host. From that night, I understood that it wasn't my perception, it wasn't my fault, and no, I wasn't *"too sensitive."*

Many of us need a few slaps to react, but you know what? That's okay... we all have to go through our own process.

The good thing is that one of those necessary slaps gives us enough momentum to get to the next steps: to find resources, to gain strength, and to leave.

We all stay longer than we should. Not because we're stupid, but because we were hooked by hope. Hoping it would get better. Hoping they'd finally see us. Hoping that the version of them from the beginning, the one who made us feel special, alive, chosen, would return.

And that hope? It's a reflection of your capacity to believe in love. To believe in people. To believe in second chances.

But at some point, something shifts. That hope begins to crack. Not because you've given up on love, but because you've started to remember yourself. You begin to see that you deserve more than breadcrumbs, more than confusion, more than the endless loop of hoping someone will stop hurting you.

And **that's where freedom begins.** Not with rage, not even with clarity at first, but with release. You stop waiting for them to change, and start imagining a life where you get to breathe. A life where peace isn't a rare moment, but your new baseline.

Opening your eyes feels like a huge dopamine hit, right? But this one will last...

That's why it is key to learn how to **redirect** all that energy, from anger and revenge *to a* **clever plan to leave.** And from there, to **healing.**

*Come on, darling. We got this.*

## FLIPPING THE OMELETTE

In Spain, we say that referring to the traditional Spanish potato omelette. We flip it to cook it on both sides but, when one side is burnt, we flip it to show the side that looks better. We say that when a situation turns upside down. When luck changes teams. And now, **it is on yours.**

The fact that you are becoming fully aware of the type of person you are with is a **huge step**. It's the beginning of preparation, of new decisions, and the beginning of you, blooming again.

That *slap*. When you realize it's not about fixing them anymore. It's about rescuing *you*.

And no, you don't need to have it all figured out. You don't need to be *"fully healed."* You just need to *believe* that the side you haven't lived yet, the one without walking on the eggshells, without the begging, the silence, the guilt, might actually be **golden**.

## YOUR FIRE ISN'T GONE. IT WAS DIMMED

Narcissists love dimming your glow. They feed on it first. Then they fear it. When you remember your light, when you let that fire come back, they lose control.

You stop engaging. You stop justifying their behavior. You start imagining a life without them. And it doesn't feel like a weight anymore.

So if you're here, reading this… congratulations…The flip is already happening.

## AND NOW... WHAT?

**Note:** If you feel that leaving your partner is dangerous, or that staying is a potential risk, please, seek professional help immediately.

I am going to tell you how I see it and feel it... Maybe you'll agree.

Let me give you some context:

Imagine you were ready to move to Brazil. You had your plans, your life. But someone appeared: charming, seemingly aligned in values, lifestyle, even sex. They said they were changing, evolving, that they wanted what you wanted. So you stayed. **MISTAAAAAKE!!**

Months later, the truth surfaced: different values, incompatible desires, broken agreements. And your boundaries?...

### Being pushed

And there's a magnificent detail... It's NOT because *"it doesn't work"*... it's not *"misalignment."* It's the simple fact that they were lying! It was all fake!

When you get to that "Aha! moment," you are already living with a bunch of consequences... Those consequences are **debt.**

Not yours, honey... **theirs.**

[You] *Wait what?*

[Me] *Darling, there's nothing to wait and nothing to what. It is what it is.*

*They owe you.*

I left Barcelona, I left Seville, I left Lanzarote, I left Portland... all a dance of escaping and being hovered back.

Every time I escaped, I didn't only leave a place, I also left friends, opportunities, new visions that got trapped again… All those times, I wasn't really ready to go. And there is something in common: I always felt hope. I trusted, I made my real best effort, but the other side chose to lie and manipulate so, **all that loss, is debt.** It is something happening because of the choice of manipulating you from one side of the relationship.

When the omelette is flipped is when you truly know that there is no hope. You now understand that what you are feeling is not real love, and clearly start seeing the game behind the scenes.

**I understood that I was owed.** Owed years of my life, experiences, projects, cities, friendships, and ultimately, true love. I also understood, that escaping meant *leaving without being ready*, and I wasn't willing to escape anymore. I decided to prepare, to take my time, put my own pieces together, and to leave, knowing that this time, was *the good one.*

If your circumstances require urgency and you need to escape, look ahead, prepare a place to land… Find help, resources, tell people that truly love you what you are going through.

But if you need time to leave, you can start moving towards preparing a new environment to land in.

And here is where the debt comes in. Any resources given by PS to support LEAVING not escaping, are yours. You have paid in advance. Stop thinking *you are taking advantage* because it's not true. Enough of you losing. You are taking a fraction of what is already yours.

**Important Note:** Darling, hold your unicorns!! Don't sue me… I am not advising you to empty the joint bank account, okay? Or to do something illegal. What I mean by *resources* are the things that they brought into the relationship, and you can benefit from them while you get ready to go. Leave the accounts for the lawyers, sweetie!

## GIVE BACK TO THE COMMUNITY

It's normal that after opening your eyes, you feel like *this sweetie is on fire…* But darling,

**hold your unicorns!**

If you give back, try giving back to the community, not taking revenge on your ex!

If you're documenting the abuse, be smart. Use it as a shield, **not as a weapon.**

As their biggest fear is exposure, your biggest priority should be safety.

Document, record, store, and use wisely.

**Don't start a war that will drain you.**

**Remember:** Leaving is not the end, healing is. Leaving is the beginning of a new empowered and beautiful life.

## FAKE HOPE

We have already talked about hope in this book, but let me be even clearer:

**your hope is not real.**

Our mind needs to simplify things, label them in order to understand reality better and faster. You know the saying *"Not everything is what it looks like"*? This is a very clear example.

Our brain can't process the complexity of T-Bond. It doesn't say, *"Oh, addiction caused by intermittent reinforcement, of course"*. It translates it in a much more simple way: **hope.**

We know that *"the pull"* is happening because your brain is waiting for the Hoovering phase, love, connection... After pain, pleasure comes, so let's just wait. That "expecting the good part of the cycle to come" is what we feel as mere hope.

This is the first thing to do once we get to awareness: To kill it. It's not real, sweetie. It's not the good hope! It's just addiction translated in a simplistic way.

**"This is not hope, and this is not love. This is bullshit"**

That is my Narci-Mantra™. I have used it a lot. Take it, transform it, create yours. And keep it as the flagship for this moment of your life.

I remember PS crying in front of me, after making a big mess. And I was thinking, *This is not hope, and this is not love. This is bullshit*. It kept me detached from the situation, and while PS was promising the stars and faking regret, my mind was asking: *What would be more effective right now, Fake-Supply or Indifference?*

Kill hope. It'll allow you to enter a layer of your mind where you can think wisely, not impulsively.

## BREAKUP GOING THROUGH!

Okay... This is a delicate moment. I really know. Maybe you are at home reading this, thinking and thinking... and click! You finally let your brain accept that *"Yes, I'm with an abuser."* But what if all this is happening while you are still with PS?

Here is when we start *navigating like pros*. Hold your anger, hold your rage, and think with your head, darling. The moment when the flip happens is a day to celebrate, even if it feels painful. Full awareness is a sign of being on the right track.

Today, if you finally accept that PS is an abuser, you must decide when it's time to go. In some cases, you can just pack your things and go. In many others, we are hooked by trauma bond, and we need to gain strength, finish projects, talk to lawyers… In that case, you have tools to navigate manipulation. "Fake Supply, Narci-AI™, Indifference, Scale of Disaster… use them to stop engaging on a daily basis… But the focus now should be on crafting a plan to leave.

For those who can just leave (which is great news) or once you're ready to:

Once you understand that your relationship is hurting you and the breakup happens, you want to avoid getting hovered again. You now know that your subconscious is wired by childhood wounds, and a toxic cycle. You know that the moment of leaving is going to be a chance for PS to hook you back.

If you have decided to leave, use the most safe/effective method to do it. If you feel you won't resist, use a text message and close communication. If you need to do it in person, *become ice.* At least for a while…

Go through the situation and one day you will look back and **be proud of yourself.**

It's time to look out for yourself.

## ♕ ACTION STEPS

Come on, let's get creative. Let's write some Narci-Mantras™ and make them a mental tattoo.

[If you put them on your skin, please, I need to see that]

.................................................................................................................

.................................................................................................................

.................................................................................................................

.................................................................................................................

.................................................................................................................

.................................................................................................................

When are we leaving, sweetie? [Anxiety Rush] What are your initial thoughts about it? Let's think and journal for a bit. Breathe, think with your head. Look for "*Golden Hooks*." It's normal to feel a rush, but we got this, okay? Nobody is pressuring you. You're allowed to take your time, okay?

.................................................................................................................

.................................................................................................................

.................................................................................................................

.................................................................................................................

.................................................................................................................

.................................................................................................................

Narci-Mantra™! Let's create affirmations to keep us out of engagement. Make affirmations for different situations. For example:

When a conflict starts: *"There we go with the theater. None of PS's words are real. This is FAKE. PS is FAKE"*

When you miss them after a discard: *"This is not missing, not hoping... it's just the pull"*

Let's create your own:

........................................................................................................

........................................................................................................

........................................................................................................

........................................................................................................

........................................................................................................

........................................................................................................

## ◎ KEY TAKEAWAYS

✫ "The Flip" is the moment you realize that the constant confusion and "connect the dots" game is actually manipulation.

✫ This breakthrough is a huge step that marks the beginning of your preparation to leave and rescue yourself.

✫ The hope you once had begins to crack, not because you've given up on love, but because you've remembered that you deserve more than breadcrumbs.

✫ When you realize you were deceived and that the abuser owes you for the time and opportunities you lost, you can use that "debt" as fuel to prepare a safe exit plan.

✫ Kill hope.

# CHAPTER 12

# THE TWO WAYS OUT

There are only two ways a relationship with a PS ends: either they discard you, or you walk away like fire (either escaping or leaving, fire is there, I promise). Both roads hurt, but both will lead you back to yourself.

Sometimes, the ending comes suddenly and brutally. One day, you're sharing dreams and planning weekends. The next, you're blocked, replaced, or erased as if you were never there. When they discard you, they do it fast, cold, and calculated. And it breaks you. Not because you weren't aware of the pain, but because deep inside, you still had hope. That maybe, they would change. That the person you met at the beginning would come back. That love would be enough.

After a discard, what hurts most isn't just the absence and the withdrawal… it's the way they rewrite the story. Publicly, they become the victim or the hero. Privately, they *"move on"* with unsettling speed. And you're left questioning whether any of it was real. The answer is yes. It was real *for you*. That's enough. What they showed you wasn't love, it was a cycle of control, of admiration, addiction, and ego.

The moment you became less useful, they discarded you like a tool they no longer needed. This happens when you don't provide enough supply anymore, and somehow, it could be for the best.

Leaving them on your own terms is harder in a different way. You still care. You still feel connected. You still ask yourself if maybe this time, it could work. But something inside you begins to change. It's slow, but steady. You stop laughing at their painful jokes. You stop excusing the comments that make you shrink. You start noticing how exhausted you feel, how lost you've become, how loud your inner voice is but how quiet the real one has become...

You start preparing without even realizing it. You create emotional distance. You imagine yourself away from them. Maybe it takes months or years. Maybe it's after the 100th lie, or the 1,000th apology. But one day, your decision is made. Even if you don't act immediately, the fire has returned.

And sometimes, once they sense the flip, they try to get ahead of it. They discard you before you can leave, just to maintain the illusion of control. But even then... **you've still won.** Because the decision had already been made inside of you.

Whether you were discarded or you walked away, both paths leave you with a wound. There is grief. There is anger. There is confusion. And maybe still, a strange kind of love (T-Bond).

Please remember this: Staying keeps you spinning in their orbit. Being away brings you back to solid ground. It doesn't matter if you were discarded or you took the lead.

Leaving is not a one-time action. It's a process. And it begins with reclaiming your truth, your worth, and your voice, even if it's shaky. Even if you cry the whole way out, darling. That's still power.

# 👑 ACTION STEPS

**If You Were Discarded:**

- Go no contact. That includes social media. That includes mutual friends who want to play "neutral."

- Remind yourself that your pain is valid. Being thrown away doesn't make you disposable; you have a beautiful life ahead. It makes them careless and way too confident.

**If You Took the Lead:**

- Acknowledge the courage it took. Even if nobody else claps for you.

- Set a ritual to mark your departure: delete, block, cleanse, unfollow. Make space.

- Create a list of the truths that woke you up, so that when the doubt creeps in, you have something to hold onto.

**If You're In Between:**

- Start planning. Not from fear, **but from strategy**. You're not escaping (unless you need to!) You're preparing.

- Keep a journal of emotional moments and red flags. Don't let your brain gaslight you into forgetting. (Keep it safe!)

- Focus on building your next landing pad: people, space, safety.

— You may not feel strong yet, but just being here, just reading this, means something inside you has already shifted. Whether they pushed you away or you decided to walk, you're moving. And movement is power.

— You may not recognize yourself right now, but one day, you'll look back and see: This wasn't the end of your story. This was the beginning of you shining again. This time, more than ever.

## ◎ KEY TAKEAWAYS

☆ There are only two ways a relationship with a "PS" ends: They discard you, or you take the lead and leave.

☆ Being discarded is brutal, but it means you've stopped serving their ego, which is an escape.

☆ Leaving on your own terms is harder because you still care, but it is a powerful act of reclaiming your truth and voice.

☆ Regardless of how it ends, both paths lead to grief and confusion, but one keeps you in their orbit, and the other brings you back to solid ground.

☆ The journey of leaving is a process, and just the decision to leave is a sign that your power has returned.

# CHAPTER 13

# PROTECT YOURSELF

Unfortunately, the *"game"* doesn't end up with a breakup. PS normally try to either hoover you back or hurt you as revenge for abandoning them. *"Hurt you"* covers a pretty wide repertoire of possibilities. So far, we've talked a lot about how they'll attack your image, but that is the "standard," or basic move, sweetie... You may also need to protect yourself legally, financially, emotionally...

And this is a question I've received a few times: *When do I need to protect myself?*

**Ideally before leaving the relationship, escaping, or being definitively discarded.**

**If you are discarded:** The initial stage will likely be hurting you, followed by a second stage of hoovering.

**If you take the lead and leave:** Probably the initial stage will be to try hoovering you back and then (we cannot predict exactly when) a second stage of rage, trying to hurt you...

And these stages can last for a long time. So, let's think strategically and be prepared emotionally, financially, and logistically. We've got this!

Do you remember when I said in the second chapter... *Flying Monkeys?*

*"**Messages through people:** They know very well how to handle every single one of the people around them... and you. They know which of your friends or family members will spread the message, in order to hurt you, isolate you, or socially distort your image, but also, which of your loved ones can touch your heart and convince you of something. They will use this to either get a message to you, damage your image (and polish theirs), or entice you back... It's time to activate a big filter.*

Very likely, that behavior is going to intensify the moment you get away from PS, and they will **use** people in different ways. (All the participants are just victims, so control your anger, my dear). Some people will be used to **extract information**, and it can be very subtle. Maybe you don't even know that they've had a talk with PS... Some others will be used to spread gossip. Sometimes that information can be key for a legal strategy they are crafting, so let's keep this in mind, okay?

## WHEN DEFINITIVE DISCARD COMES

If you find out or figure out that you are going to be discarded, or it has already happened, you should protect yourself *immediately.* If you have properties, financial bonds, friends in common, a dog, children... You may need a lawyer, a therapist, or whatever you consider necessary in order to stay protected and ready.

In this stage of rage, they will try to use your people and the people you may have in common to hurt you.

You may want talk to your friends and family and maybe say something like:

*"Hey, I'm getting out of a very difficult relationship with _____ where I have felt abused, and it is very likely that they will contact you in*

*order to send a message. Please, I need to ask you to stay away from that topic/to not engage/not to tell me anything that _____ shares"*

Maybe you'll need to disconnect from some people or say something like: *"This is a delicate situation and I won't share any information for now, but remember that I love you."* You will also have people trying to get information, so beware.

In this scenario, you may need to take care of the logistics of separating from this person, and also legal and financial matters at the same time. **They will take action so, you do the same.**

## WHEN YOU TAKE THE LEAD

If they start a hoovering phase, they will use people to extract information. They will also cry and even admit part of their trash to your people, especially to the ones who might influence you. So plan on talking to them. Limit the *Flying Monkeys*.

In this possible scenario, you may win some time.

**They are not going to hurt you while trying to hoover you back.**

So logistics are first, either moving away or kicking their ass out.

But don't get too comfortable! Because as soon as PS realizes that there's no possibility of reconciliation, a new phase of rage may start. That means, even if you have more time, **protect yourself.**

(More in the next chapter)

## ♔ ACTION STEPS

We know that they plan ahead, but so do you:

Identify possible chinks in your armor. Think about the bonds you have with PS. People, finances, valuables…

.......................................................................................................................

.......................................................................................................................

.......................................................................................................................

.......................................................................................................................

Start crafting an initial plan in your head, or on paper or in the notes app of your phone!

What are the most urgent/important things to take care of? What things can wait?

.......................................................................................................................

.......................................................................................................................

.......................................................................................................................

.......................................................................................................................

.......................................................................................................................

.......................................................................................................................

.......................................................................................................................

.......................................................................................................................

.......................................................................................................................

We are not going to start *"spiralizing"*, but we want to be ahead of the circumstances, just like somebody else you know is… So, if some of the important people and things are affected, what will you do?

.................................. ...................................................................

............................................. ...........................................................

................................................ ........................................................

.................................... ...............................................................

.................................................. ......................................................

............................................. .........................................................

.............................. ............................................................................

.................................................. ......................................................

## ◎ KEY TAKEAWAYS

⭐ The "game" does not end with the breakup; the narcissist will either try to hoover you back or seek revenge.

⭐ You must be strategically prepared emotionally, financially, and logistically to protect yourself during and after the separation.

⭐ They will use mutual friends and family to extract information, spread gossip, and manipulate the people around you.

⭐ A key part of your strategy is to talk to your trusted people, inform them of the abuse, and ask them not to engage with the abuser or relay messages.

⭐ Seeking professional support from a team of beautiful people (therapists, lawyers, and anyone else you might need) is a very effective way to stay protected and have your hand held.

# CHAPTER 14

# THE INFO-SHIELD™

**Note:** This chapter is oriented to the scenario of PS wanting to stay in the relationship and you needing prep time.

*We want to run away from pain. Once we know who we are with, we tend to escape as soon as possible. We are in such pain that we might make decisions that will generate even more pain in the future. It is important to stop for a minute and think…*

This means… **enough of you losing.**

We talked about leaving vs. escaping, but even when you decide to take some time in order to leave, unicorns pull…

The more aware and mentally prepared you are for dealing with a narcissist, the more you will want to leave… But what if you cannot afford to live alone right now? What if for some reason you don't have anywhere to go right now? What if you have stuff you need to take care of before leaving? What if you just need to figure out how to make the big move back to being single after being with a narcissist, and you need time?

We know how breaking up with PS might affect your life, so I'm going to give you some ideas and summarize some others in order to contain the damage after leaving.

The goal of this chapter is to teach you how to create what I call an Info-Shield™. I'm going to guide you through one possible scenario, but the possibilities are immense…

## THE FIRST (CLEVER) MOVE...

(I told you to be very careful when documenting events of abuse. Please keep that in mind.)

We know that we are in a cycle, so we already expect that devaluation and discards are coming. But this time, we are ahead…

We need time to pick up the pieces of our life before leaving, and that could be one week, one month… or six. Believe me, in that time you'll go through the cycle at least once, but this time, our communication is going to change slightly. We are going to push them into sending text messages instead of so many phone calls or in-person communication during your next conflict. Say you need distance. Maybe you just go for a "decompressing walk," and while you are away, you send them a text…

Also, record calls secretly in moments of "you trying to be understood"… In many jurisdictions, they don't have legal value. Please check how it is in yours. If you can legally (and safely) record to document abuse…

Do it.

Let's go deeper with a real case study:

## [Phone Call]

> [PS] *I don't know why you're upset about me leaving with that guy from the bar. It was just fun, nothing serious.* (+ PS's Bar Classic Combo 2 + 3 + 5…)

[Us] *Okay… but if I left with someone in front of you, would that feel fine to you?*

[PS] *You're exaggerating. You always compare things that aren't the same.* (+ PS's Bar Classic Combo 1 + 4…) [This is PS trying to protect a Funnel Agreement]

[Us] *I need to step back for now. Let's continue later. I'm not okay.* [Fake Supply, darling]

[After ten minutes — Texting — Fake-Supply + Narci-Form™]

[Us – Text 1] *I feel you're not addressing my concern, so please take your time to read this and answer clearly.*

[Us – Text 2] 1: *Would you feel comfortable if I openly left with someone else at a bar in front of you? 2: If yes, then no problem, now we're aligned. But if it would hurt you, shouldn't you just acknowledge that instead of minimizing it? 3: If not, why are you defending your own behavior? Thank you. I'll be waiting for your answers.*

Do not answer the phone, honey, because it's going to ring. Force them to reply via text. Block communication until they answer your questions via text. This scenario fits very well with their self-made concept of you being unstable and controlling, so we are going to use it in our favor, and they will probably reply.

You may receive something like this:

[Text from PS] *Thanks for writing it down. 1: I don't want us to make rules about flirting with others that would box us in. 2: What matters to me is that we have trust, love, and support — that's what you deserve. 3:* [No answer.]

Again, they are not answering our questions. So you can drop it here, being aware of it, or push a bit more by saying: "None of this answers my actual questions. You're putting it back on me." And they'll keep using some more PS's Classic Combos... maybe even give you a little bit of truth. Don't stay here eternally if you need time; just drop it eventually — but remember, hold your unicorns!

[You] *Daniel, WTF is this for?*

[Me] *Sweetie, you just legally documented signs of emotional abuse...*

**Let me give you another useful real case study:**

**[Morning — PS is calling after a fight last night. We don't answer.]**

**[Text Messages]**

**[PS]** *Hey, I've been trying to reach you...*

**[Us]** *I'm exhausted. Yesterday I opened up about how invisible I feel when you ignore me, and instead of reassurance, you just said I was "too sensitive."*

**[PS]** *I think we had a slight misunderstanding there: "Sensitive" vs. "sensible." I didn't mean you're "too sensitive" (as in overreacting). What I meant was "sensible," like you pay close attention to details, which can sometimes make you feel things more strongly. That's what I was trying to express yesterday.*

No more is needed, darling. With this move, we have done two things.

**The first one:** With this answer, PS is admitting not taking care of your feelings yesterday.

**The second one:** One more time, they are avoiding accountability with manipulation techniques, not focusing on your feelings or being real today.

One more piece of evidence in our Narci-Box™…

So from now on, until the day we leave, we are going to do this "First (Clever) Move," okay? All possible conflicts will leave a written trace.

**Note:** Never, NEVER, DARLING, share when all this started, not even after breaking up. This information is yours. If one day you need evidence, they won't even imagine when it all started inside of you. This is the first thing they'll need to know. Don't give them that pleasure. They'll want to know, and they will think "they have been taking advantage of me' and use it against you.

Please, don't get entertained by this, and do not stay longer than necessary. **Please.**

## BACK TO EXPOSURE

Remember I said they fear being exposed? And I recommended not doing it…

But what if their fear itself is used as a tool?

**[emoji sunglasses]**

Let's talk about exposure in a different way. Not public exposure, darling! But exposure between you and PS. A clever and elaborate way of saying, *"I not only saw you… I also caught you."*

What I'm about to teach you is a badass technique that has to be used very carefully (please!) and requires keeping your unicorns on a very short leash… One more time, this is not a tool to stay longer, but to leave safely, okay?

Now that we all are clear that we are going to use their fear of exposure, but not publicly expose them (for now, we'll get there later), let's take a look at two types of exposure:

**Open Exposure and Radical Exposure (always between you and PS only!)**

## OPEN EXPOSURE

Let me be very real… this might be useful in some cases, but it can be problematic. I am explaining this to you so you either use it in a clever and studied way, or you learn what not to do.

Open Exposure means telling them openly "I have proof of your abuse," but you are not fully shielded. You are still open to pain. The shield is not strong enough yet. In some cases, it might be enough to contain future damage, but in some others it will look like a provocation and generate conflicts and/or painful discards.

You might be tempted to do something like the following examples. Do it only after considering this is the best way to go, or else avoid it.

Please, if you decide to do this, do it only when you are ready to go… Otherwise, avoid it!

Here we go…

Let's open our dear Narci-AI™ and let's type this prompt:

*Hi Narci… I'm sad. This is what happened [give it context]… so I tried to get understanding in a phone call, and as it was impossible, I sent PS a text… These are the questions and answers: [copy and paste the text messages]. Can you find signs of manipulation or emotional abuse in these texts?*

## Real case study: [Narci-AI™ answers...]

Question 1:
*"Would you feel comfortable if I openly left with someone else at a bar in front of you?"*

His response:
*"Thanks for writing it down. I don't want us to make rules about flirting that would box us in."*

What's happening: Deflection + Emotional Redirection. (He avoids yes/no and reframes it as you trying to control him, not his actions.)

Question 2:
*"If yes, then no problem, now we're aligned. But if it would hurt you, shouldn't you just acknowledge that instead of minimizing it?"*

His response:
*"What matters to me is that we have trust, love, and support — that's what you deserve."*

What's happening: Future-Faking + Emotional Fogging. (He replaces a direct answer with dreamy words to avoid accountability.)

Question 3:
*"If not, why are you defending your own behavior?"*

His response:
[No answer.]

What's happening: Deliberate Vagueness + Withholding.

Six manipulation techniques in three sentences. How productive.

Now imagine that your wild unicorns make you copy all this Narci-AI™ response, paste it in a text adding "you are a manipulator"… and boom… send it…

Don't expect anything good, sweetie…

This is an Open Exposure example. Let me give you another one:

### Real case study: [In person]

> [We] *I recorded when you were screaming and banging the door to make me get out the other day. I have also been recording and documenting things for a while now… I don't want to do anything with it, so just leave me alone forever.*
>
> [PS] *Since when?!* [New obsession unlocked]
>
> [We] *I don't have anything else to say.*
>
> [PS leaves the house]

Risky, darling… Maybe effective, but ugh…

Let's go to a safer, shielded version of exposure that you may want to consider…

**Note:** They will want to know when you started crafting a plan, or playing their game in a more clever way than them. They'll try to guess what evidence you have.

They are the ones giving, not you taking.

They'll accuse you of taking advantage of them.

Their knowing when it all started is not good for you, sweetie pie.

## RADICAL EXPOSURE - SEALING THE INFO-SHIELD™

The goal is to use it only once. The day you are fully ready to go and everything is prepared for your transition to your new life.

Let's breathe… I know, sweetie. We got this, remember.

Check out this real case scenario:

**Step 1: [Email]**

*Hi,*

*I've tried many times to explain how your behavior has affected me because I was hoping for change. It didn't work…*

*After speaking with licensed professionals and reviewing our message history, I've been advised to prioritize my well-being, keep written records, and step back. I'm not looking for a fight; I'm following professional guidance and taking care of myself.*

*From now on, please keep any necessary logistics in writing only. I won't be discussing the relationship further.*

*I'll remember the good moments.*

*Take care.*

**Boom…**

**Step 2: [5 minutes after the email —
Text message to a group chat with common friends + PS]**

*Goodbye, my sweet friends…For now I'm stepping back and focusing on recovery from narcissistic patterns. I am grateful to count on PS's support on my journey. It's been a long road, and I'm grateful for the beautiful moments we shared. Hoping I'll see you soon, guys.*

*Love, ...................................................*

Okay, so we have one message announcing to people who probably love you a breakup… with the word **narcissistic** in it…

Do you remember the breadcrumbs, sweetie? What about the "Never Connecting Dots"?

Do you know what can make people connect the dots?

**PS's shit talk.**

The worse they talk about you, the more people will start looking with different eyes…

The goal of making this move? To contain, not to hurt.

Now it's in their hands… if they are clever enough, they'll reach that conclusion by themselves. And if not, they will hurt themselves. Narcissists fail. It's just a matter of time. Until now, they've relied on people's ignorance (on others not knowing, not suspecting) to move guilt-free. But now, things are different.

**Important notes:** The person who generously shared this case study was:

★ Legally protected.
★ Emotionally supported by licensed therapists.
★ Following professional advice, not just Narci-AI™…

This strategy makes hoovering almost impossible, shields you, and provides a legal safety net in case things get worse…

Once you get here, it's time to let the shield do the work, put away the Narci-Box™, breathe… and start looking forward to an amazing future.

I love you; we got this.

# ♛ ACTION STEPS

Can you find evidence in your text threads? Please, take a look only if you still need it. Did you find any? What does Narci-AI™ say about them?

.......................................................................................................................

.......................................................................................................................

.......................................................................................................................

.......................................................................................................................

.......................................................................................................................

.......................................................................................................................

.......................................................................................................................

So, you can just take your things and go (or kick PS's ass out), you can create an Info-Shield™, or you can get support from a therapist while you're in this complex process of leaving. What do you think would work best for you — going naked, going super protected, or somewhere in the middle? To consider this, think about "how dangerous PS will be."

.......................................................................................................................

.......................................................................................................................

.......................................................................................................................

.......................................................................................................................

.......................................................................................................................

.......................................................................................................................

What are the next steps then?

........................................................................................

........................................................................................

........................................................................................

........................................................................................

........................................................................................

........................................................................................

........................................................................................

........................................................................................

........................................................................................

## ◎ KEY TAKEAWAYS

★ Taking "prep time" to leave safely is a valid and necessary strategy, especially when you need to secure financial or personal resources. The goal is to contain damage and gain time, not to lose more.

★ The "Info-Shield™" is a strategy to document emotional abuse in writing to use later for legal and personal protection. This involves pushing conflicts into written communication, such as text messages, to create a paper trail.

★ The "First (Clever) Move" is a tactic to strategically ask questions in writing that force the narcissist to either admit to their manipulative behavior or reveal their avoidance tactics. This provides "legal documentation" and evidence for your "Narci-Box™".

★ "Open Exposure" is risky. Be very careful with your own impulses after gathering evidence; we tend to tell them what we have uncontrollably. Use your bullets effectively.

★ "Radical Exposure" is a one-time, shielded strategy to use when you are ready to leave. It involves informing the narcissist that you have documented evidence of abuse, which can act as a shield against their future manipulation and make hoovering almost impossible.

★ This strategy is a safety net, not a tool for revenge, and should only be used after you are legally protected, emotionally supported by licensed therapists, and have followed professional advice.

# CHAPTER 15

# REVENGE IS SUPPLY!

*"Never wrestle with a pig. You both get dirty,
but it enjoys the mud."*

Don't you love the multiple Spanish sayings about pigs?

**Note:** This chapter isn't about legal justice. It's about the urge for personal revenge, which can backfire hard. If you're facing real danger, please seek professional or legal help.

**Revenge**

=

MISTAKE!

Does PS deserve it? If you believe so, then I believe you. Is it normal to have those feelings?

**Totally**

But is it a good idea?

**No**

## THE DARK FORCES

I thought everybody learned while growing up "you gotta be good," "you gotta be nice," but the raw reality is that it is not true. Some people live in the dimension of Dark Forces, lying, cheating, manipulating, being cruel. It is their comfort zone, not yours (fortunately). They enjoy conflict... they enjoy the mud.

They have become who they are over many years. Their Dark Powers are part of their DNA (just like Glow is in ours). We tend to plan our next move and visualize the consequence. A narcissist goes beyond and, believe me, will reply back.

On the other hand, they plan the next move, then, not just the consequence, but your reaction, what your probable next move would look like, how it will impact them, and how they will reply. And they are pretty good at that. Their mind always works ahead.

The impact and risks this can have for you are unexpected.

## THE "ENEMY" IS AT HOME

Think about this: what is more painful?

- If you go home and, when you get in, your partner doesn't say hello and ignores you? Or if your neighbor doesn't say hello and ignores you?

- If you go to the bakery and the cashier talks rudely to you, or if your partner, a good friend, or a family member does?

Most of the pain we suffer in life comes from people who, for many possible reasons, "matter." People who, along the way, breached the walls of your heart: "your home."

If we add the fact that the person hurting you is also a narcissist, then the pain increases exponentially. Just because you left PS, it doesn't mean they're out of your system. That happens when indifference moves in, and that is the moment of real (and effective) revenge.

## AN UNDERLYING MESSAGE

As you know now, their supply is your attention, and more importantly, your insecurity, your rage… the control over your feelings. Acts of revenge are sending this message: "Yes, you are angry, because I can make you angry." "You are raging because I still have that power over you." While you are executing your "great planned move"… they are laughing…

Your rage says: *"You still matter."*
Your silence says: *"You don't exist."*

## JUST LIKE A PIECE OF CARDBOARD

As I said, indifference is the real revenge and the real way to cut off completely from a narcissist. We are not going to get there with the goal of revenge, but with the goals of getting rid of this person, and **being** able to heal. As a consequence, that will hurt them.

Also, 'hurting on purpose' is their style, not ours. We're not here to play their game, we're here to win by walking away. You don't have to wait to be fully healed in order to start showing indifference. Go zero contact as soon as you can. Yes, they may rage. Yes, they may try to bait you. But without your reactions, they'll get bored and vanish. That's not revenge, that's freedom. Your healing process will run in parallel, and indifference will become more natural each time. The more you practice indifference, and control yourself **not** to engage, the easier it becomes.

These are the two things that helped me personally. (This is not psychological advice, but survivor testimony)

* Imagining that PS is just a piece of cardboard. Something insignificant... Before, that box held important things. But once I emptied it, I broke it down, and tossed it in the recycling bin. Now it's just... cardboard.

  Ugh, that sounds rough, but it is something that helped me!

* Do you remember all those moments when PS ignored you? Do you remember how it felt? You want them to feel exactly the same way.

  I know... it invokes vengeful feelings, but honestly, back in the day I wanted revenge! I had those feelings! So understanding that not taking action for revenge works way better... helped me to "stay in indifference." (Faking it until I made it... and I did make it! And you are getting there too).

## BREAKING FREE FROM REVENGE

Over time, those feelings will fade. For a while, they come and go, and I remembered and repeated like a mantra, "Just don't do anything... don't even react... My reaction is their win, their dopamine hit." And I also said to myself, "It's okay, my love... it's okay." Sometimes I still do. And that's okay...

Treat yourself with compassion, allow the feelings to go through and then process them. Healing is not about burying feelings, but about processing them over time and with some work. We'll talk more about this in the next section of this book.

# ♛ ACTION STEPS

If staying indifferent is hard right now, try a few "Cardboard Techniques" or self-dialogs and see how your body reacts. See if your feelings become more gentle or stay the same. Try to find something that works for you, to be able to show indifference and stay there, until it starts happening naturally.

Write down your own script, your own mantra, to repeat when triggered.

........................................... ............................................................

............................................................................................................

............................................................................................................

........................................... ...............................................................

............................................................................................................

............................................................................................................

............................................................................................................

........................................... ...............................................................

........................................... ...............................................................

## 🎯 KEY TAKEAWAYS

★ Seeking revenge is a mistake because a narcissist lives in the "dimension of Dark Forces" and enjoys conflict.

★ Your rage and desire for revenge are a form of supply for them, sending the message that they still have power over you.

★ The real revenge is indifference; it's the most effective way to cut them off because it denies them the supply they crave.

★ Indifference becomes easier over time, with practice and a focus on healing yourself.

★ You can fake indifference until it becomes a natural part of your healing process.

**Find me on the other side!**

www.thesparkletrap.com/qr5

# BYEEEEE!

*"Going down the layers of my feelings,*
*I saw anger,*
*I saw rage,*
*guilt, frustration...*
*and the dead hope I used to hold on to.*
*But going down,*
*more and more,*
*I found it...*
*Vertigo,*
*that feeling of being about to jump off a cliff...*
*Vertigo,*
*filling the gap that fake hope left...*
*Vertigo,*
*that feeling of the unknown...*

*Fear of change..."*

There's a moment when feelings shift inside of us. Now we deal with uncertainty, with fear of change and fear of consequences. But let me be very direct, my love: we can deal with it, okay? It's hard, but we've got this... it is a moment to put on unicorn blinders.

**Just look ahead.**

**Forget about the noise, push away your fear.**

**There's a new and much better reality waiting for you.**

It's time to say…

Byeeeee!

CHAPTER 16

# A LETTER NOT
# TO BE SENT

That's it. That's the letter I would send a narcissist after leaving—the one I would put on the living room table. Great, right? I mean... why are we going to spend more energy explaining things they never intended to understand?! (Meaning your feelings.) For a narcissist, your feelings are just meant to be flipped, gaslit, minimized, and weaponized.

If after breaking up you feel the need to send a "mic drop" message, save yourself the trouble. Do not give them the gift of information. Do not give them the gift of **KNOWING**. Now, your inner world is yours, and only yours—keep it like that. Remember, anything they know will be used against you.

Such a note can be good to write, but not to send. In my case, this is what my note would have looked like:

*Ex-Dear Piece of Shit (PS):*

*You told me we were on the same page. We weren't. You never were. I've seen the person you hide: the lies, the performative charm, the manipulations. It's not about revenge—it's that I can't unsee what I learned. I tried to make you understand for us. I tried to be real. You called it weakness.*

*I've kept records. I've asked for help. I'm not here to start a fight. I'm closing this chapter and protecting myself. Cross my name off your contacts list and move on. Don't reply; I won't even send it! I'm stepping into healing. You can keep the parties and the distractions. I hope you one day stop causing pain. For everyone's sake, stay single until you do the work and achieve proven results...*

*(Good luck with that.)*

*Wishing you nothing—not good, not bad—I won't even spend energy on that.*

*Daniel*

*P.S. I'm sorry this is your only source of self-esteem... but not even with a pallet of Cialis will you be XL.*

**[emoji sunglasses]**

[PS] *OMG Daniel, you're raging...*

[My brain, thinking something I wouldn't actually say] *I expected you here. I knew you wouldn't close the book at the beginning.*

*Now you're the one who needs to know. And now... I just don't care.*

[Me] *To my dear queer, beautiful soul reading this book and needing support:*

- We are allowed to rage.
- We are allowed to let it out.
- And believe me...
- We can let it go.

# ♕ ACTION STEPS

Let's go… write that letter. **NEVER SEND IT.** But let's put on paper what's already in that beautiful mind. Let it out, see it with your eyes… and then burn it, throw it away, or flush it! Remember, you don't need closure from them. **You are the closure.**

Please don't leave the letter somewhere visible, darling… we are not creating a weapon to be used against ourselves!

I remember perfectly the day I said EVERYTHING I had been keeping bottled up inside. And I felt heard by a loved one—and not judged. When I said it, and I heard, "It's okay, hon, it's normal…" Wow. A big weight in my belly got released (I'm not talking about Spanish tapas!).

Today I invite you to say it out loud! Even if you're alone, LET IT OUT, darling! I'm here to tell you: it's okay, babe… it's normal you feel that way (and you have all those dark desires that you'll never execute, right? Darling, hold your unicorns).

## 🎯 KEY TAKEAWAYS

★ You do not need to send a long, detailed breakup letter to a narcissist because they will use it to gaslight, minimize, and flip the script.

★ A letter full of your feelings gives them valuable information they don't deserve.

★ Writing a letter for yourself is a powerful exercise to release your feelings and gain clarity, but it should be burned or thrown away afterward.

★ Remember that you are the closure—you don't need it from them.

# CHAPTER 17

# THE ZERO CONTACT CLUB

*Going zero contact is not just a boundary, it's a breakthrough.*

For most people, zero contact means blocking, deleting, and never speaking again. But for us, the queer community, it's not always that simple (unless it's necessary or worth it to change cities).

We live in tight-knit communities. We may share bars, clubs, friends, or even lovers! We're a web of chosen family, exes, and future flings. So what do you do when PS keeps showing up at your favorite bar, or when mutual friends keep inviting you both to the same birthday or pool party?!?

## FIRST THINGS FIRST

Sweetie, let me be very real with you, and this is not what you'll normally hear on YouTube…

**We are humans. Yeah. Not machines.**

After breaking up with PS, you'll want to look at your phone to somehow connect. You'll want to check Instagram stories, or go through your "Detective Mode" tools trying to find a message to see if they are as affected as you.

Now, we know they're not, right? It's normal, my love... and it's okay that you want to know about someone you were so invested in... it's natural and human. So stop judging and torturing yourself, okay?

Am I saying it's okay to do it? No. But probably you will.

Think about it: from drama to silence...

It sounds good, but your subconscious mind is freaking out. You're missing intensity, not love.

Should you try not to connect or check anything from them?

**Absolutely. And you will get there.**

## WHEN YOU CAN'T GO FULLY ZERO CONTACT

Same city, same queer bars, same community... fuck... We have it a little harder unless you change cities or countries, which is unfair too.

If you can't go 100% no contact because of social overlap, we'll set **Emotional Zero Contact**. That means:

- No reaction posts. They'll know.

- No replying. Even if they say they're dying. Even if they post something just for you to see.

- No lingering in their orbit. Don't visit their Instagram. Don't read mutuals' stories just to spot them.

- Mute is better than block if you want to avoid drama, but if you need to block — **block**.

It's hard… ugh, I know… but slowly we'll get there.

Emotional Zero Contact happens through awareness. The clearer you are that every single word out of PS's mouth is manipulation, the easier it is to pull the plug…

## TACTICAL MOVES FOR THE QUEER SCENE

Let trusted friends know you don't want to cross paths.

Be okay with skipping events if needed. Your healing is way more important than your presence.

Create your own safe spaces. Host your own dinners, game nights, queer movie nights. Rebuild connection on your terms.

If you have mutual friends who pressure you to "be civil," tell them clearly: "This is a difficult and unique situation, and it's better for you guys to stay out of it. Thank you for your support and understanding."

## IF THEY HOOVER…

A random text. A sexy story. A *"Did I see you last night?"* DM.

**Delete.**
**Do not respond.**
**Your silence is your statement.**

You are no longer a sparkle they get to trap.

## WHY ZERO CONTACT IS ESSENTIAL

Zero contact is not revenge; it's not *"I'm angry, so now I give you emotional withholding."* No.

**It's rehab.**

It's about detoxing your nervous system and protecting your clarity. Even one tiny message can reopen the wound and pull you back into confusion. We need to seal ourselves off from them as soon as we leave (or escape).

## THE AFTER-LEAVING RUSH

The After-Leaving Rush is that pinch in your belly — that rush of anxiety that happens pretty often when we get away from PS.
Every time you feel the rush and don't react, **you are slapping the bond.**
Every time you say "enough!" **it's a crack in the bond.**
And as it gets weaker, you see clearer, and you get stronger.
To disrupt the rush, I use images or characters that help give me distance from my own thoughts — like a "huge gray rock." I think about El Capitan in Yosemite. Solid, silent, but impervious. It doesn't matter how much they push… you won't even feel it.

**You're El Capitan now.**

Something that also helps is to keep clear in our minds one or two of those things that were too much. And when the rush to see if they have texted comes, or when you think about weird, illogical, destructive, not really wanted possibilities about getting back together… you must go back to those memories that represent your past and future with PS. That day locked out of the car, or that destroyed birthday party…

Don't pick something too triggering or painful… just bad enough. This is only for the first stages of dealing with trauma bonding after leaving, with that weird as fuck cocktail of feelings.

## SAD BUT HAPPY…

For a while, it's normal to still feel the effects of trauma bonding pulling back… But also, you will know that you are doing the right thing, finally and forever.

I call those days "Sad but Happy Days," and you know what, hon? Let it out… cry it out, don't punish yourself if you look at your phone to check for a message. Well, punish yourself for it if you need to, but just let it out! And also let the happy side come out! Say *"I fucking chose myself."* That's something to fucking celebrate, my love.

## THE ZERO CONTACT CLUB

There are tons of people who have gone zero contact already. Maybe only inside of themselves for now, maybe partially because they have a family to take care of (children, etc.). But many of us are in zero contact fully. We are all dealing with it the best we can, and you know what? We can provide great support for each other; it doesn't matter where you are in the process.

I created a support community where I share free resources, exclusive content, and Q&As.

Let's connect!

Scan the QR code below and join today!

**Zero Contact Club —**
**The Other Side of "The Sparkle Trap"**

www.thesparkletrap.com/community

## ♕ ACTION STEPS

—  Write a commitment letter to yourself: decide what "zero contact" means for you.

—  Create a "Zero Contact Emergency Toolkit": three things you'll do when tempted to check their profile or reply (listen to your sparkle audio, text your bestie, go outside).

—  Post this on social media or just in the feed of your mind (we are not planning to send messages through posts, okay?):*"Replying to that ex? MISTAKE!"*

## ◎ KEY TAKEAWAYS

★ Zero contact is essential for detoxing your nervous system and protecting your clarity; even a single message can reopen the wound.

★ If you can't go fully zero contact due to being in a tight-knit community, you can practice "emotional zero contact" by not replying, reacting, or lurking on their social media.

★ You can create your own safe spaces and set boundaries with mutual friends who try to pressure you into "being civil."

★ Your silence is your most powerful statement, and it proves you are no longer a "sparkle they get to trap."

# CHAPTER 18

# THE SHAME OF WANTING THEM BACK

This is the part that sucks. Missing PS doesn't mean you're stupid or that you were lying or exaggerating about the troubles that you may have shared in the past with your family or friends. That craving-for-their-attention feeling doesn't erase the pain they caused. You can know someone is toxic and still want them back, because trauma bonds don't end with logic. They untangle with time, compassion, and truth.

You were wired, over time, to associate their breadcrumbs with love. You were fed inconsistency under the name of passion. You were starved of safety and told it was your fault. And now, your nervous system doesn't know what to do without the chaos.

The shame doesn't just come from missing them — it comes from feeling like you shouldn't. You beat yourself up for checking their Instagram. You delete the text, then rewrite it. Then delete it again (don't send it!). You tell yourself, "I should be over this." But healing doesn't work on a timer.

Let's be honest: part of you still wants their love because part of you still hopes it was real. You want to believe that the connection meant something. That you weren't just a placeholder. That they're out there missing you too.

But here's the brutal truth: they're probably not. At least not in the way you hope. Narcissists don't miss you... they miss the control, the supply, the game.

So what do you do with the part of you that still longs for them? You don't shame it. You meet it — with softness, with honesty, with a reminder of how far you've come.

You remember that part:

- Yes, they made you feel special, **but only to extract.**

- Yes, you felt chosen, **but only because they needed someone to play the role.**

- Yes, there were good moments, **but they came wrapped in cruelty.**

- Craving them doesn't mean you should go back. It means you're grieving. You're mourning the dream, the fantasy, the potential. **And that grief is allowed.**

*You can hold sadness and clarity at the same time.*
*You can miss them and still choose yourself.*
*You can feel weak today and still be stronger than yesterday.*

# 👑 ACTION STEPS

– Name the craving for what it is: not love, but longing for relief, familiarity, or closure.

– When you feel the urge to contact them, write a letter you never send. Let it pour out, then burn it.

– Set a 24-hour rule before reaching out. Most urges pass when given space.

– Create a mantra: "I miss who I thought they were, not who they actually are."

– Talk to someone who sees you clearly. Let them reflect your truth back when your mind gets foggy. Give them permission — ask them for it.

– Remember what missing them cost you. Write it down if you need to. Tattoo it in your mind.

Wanting them back doesn't make you weak.

Acting on it is what reopens the wound.

You don't owe anyone a perfect healing story.

You just owe yourself this: **to not betray yourself again in the name of hope.**

Because real love — **the kind that's safe, kind, and freeing — will never ask you to abandon your truth just to keep it alive.**

## ◎ KEY TAKEAWAYS

★ It's normal to miss a narcissist and want them back, even if you know they are toxic, because trauma bonds don't end with logic.

★ You were wired to associate their inconsistent behavior with love, and your nervous system doesn't know what to do without the chaos.

★ Narcissists don't miss you; they miss the control, the supply, and the game.

★ You can hold sadness and clarity at the same time, and craving them is a sign of grieving the dream and the fantasy, not a sign you should go back.

★ You don't owe anyone a perfect healing story; you owe yourself the commitment to not betray yourself again for the sake of hope.

# CHAPTER 19

# WHY DIDN'T YOU...?!

Honestly? The *"why didn't you"* bothered me a lot at first, but then I stopped trying to get understanding from people who will never understand. I started choosing my vitamin people better. People who wouldn't judge, or who didn't even need to know the specifics. They were just there.

## THE SOCIAL PRESSURE INSIDE ABUSE

Let's talk about that wall. The one you hit when you try to speak your truth, and it bounces back.

You finally open up. You say, "I wasn't safe." And they squint, tilt their head, and ask, *"But... did they hit you?"*

You say, *"It was emotional abuse."* And they pause. *"Are you sure? PS always seemed so kind."*

You say, *"I couldn't breathe in that relationship."* And they smile gently and say, *"Relationships are hard. You have to work on them."* Ugh... angry emoji right TF now.

That's the wall. The wall that says your truth isn't enough. That unless you have bruises or police reports or a perfect timeline of horrors, then maybe... you're not a *real* victim. It's a wall built by ignorance, discomfort, and a world that still doesn't understand how deep emotional abuse cuts. A world that punishes survivors for not leaving sooner, and then doubts them when they do.

It can create this deep, painful silence, because you may start wondering…

Was it really that bad? Maybe I'm exaggerating. Maybe I should've tried harder. Maybe I'm just too sensitive.

**No, darling.** You were surviving the best way you knew how.

And your truth is enough.
   Even if it's messy,
   even if you stayed too long,
   even if no one else saw it.

If you are doubting yourself right now, ask:

- Did I feel safe in that relationship?
- Was I shrinking to stay loved?
- Did I change who I was, just to keep the peace?
- Did I stop recognizing myself?

If the answer is yes, you don't need anyone else's permission to name what happened.

You are allowed to leave. To cut ties. To go no contact. To tell your story, or to keep it private.

You are allowed to be a victim without a visible wound. You are allowed to be a survivor without anyone's validation.

When people say, *"Victims don't leave because they don't want to,"* they reveal how little they know. We stay because of trauma bonds. Because of hope. Because we were trained to doubt ourselves.

We stay because abuse messes with your reality, and that's the whole point of it.

So next time someone says, "Why didn't you just leave?"

You don't owe them a thing. Your story isn't for their comfort. It's for your liberation.

I remember many years ago, in Spain, there was a case that made news headlines: a young woman who had been kidnapped and held captive for three years. When discovered, the girl, after being rescued, wanted to go back to her captor.

Back in the day, it was normal to see opinionated people on TV criticizing everything with no compassion, basically laughing at a victim of PTSD.

That case stayed with me, not just because of her suffering, but because of how unprepared society was to understand it. It revealed something ugly: how quick people are to judge what they don't understand, especially when abuse isn't simple or visible.

Nowadays, some topics are treated with more compassion, but still, people are not ready to understand what you went through. And it's not their fault or your fault.

It doesn't feel good, but you don't have to educate people in order to get some understanding.

Even people who love you for real can be confused, and even manipulated, after your breakup with PS.

Think about this: if you have been manipulated for a long time and at the same time have seen the real side of PS, imagine how easy it is to manipulate the people around you.

Keep in mind the social armor PS created with them, with your family and friends, and the fact that normally, people are empathetic and not suspicious.

A few of their techniques are enough to manipulate your loved ones. But ultimately, those are your people, and many times they will follow your lead, even while asking you "why didn't you leave earlier if it was so bad?" or "what's wrong with…?"

Tell them that you are leaving a very toxic and difficult relationship, that you want to go zero contact, and that please, they should block or stop engaging with that person who has been actively hurting you. You do not have to answer all the questions. You do not need to share your side of the story...

**Time will.**

# ♛ ACTION STEPS

**Create a Go-To Response for Doubters:**

Prepare one clear sentence you can use when someone questions your decision or experience.

For example:

*"Things got difficult, and I did what I needed to protect my peace."*

Keep it short, neutral, and final. You don't need to debate your pain.

...................................................................................................................

...................................................................................................................

...................................................................................................................

...................................................................................................................

**Protect Your Peace with Boundaries:**

Not everyone deserves access to your story. Decide ahead of time who gets full truth, partial truth, or none. It's not lying. **It's emotional safety.**

**Turn the Spotlight Around:**

When someone asks, *"Why didn't you leave sooner?"* gently flip the question:*"Would you ask that to someone who was mugged? Or attacked?"* It invites reflection without confrontation and reminds them that abuse isn't a logic test.

Use "Gray Rock" with Nosy People:

When you can't avoid someone (family, coworkers, mutual friends), use the gray rock method: Be boring. Give short, non-emotional answers. Don't defend. Don't explain. Just let the conversation roll off you.

Keep a "Truth File":

In moments of doubt or when others question you, revisit your truth: screenshots, journal entries, things they said, things you felt. It's not for revenge — it's to remind yourself that you're not crazy, and it was real

Connect with Others Who Understand:

If your immediate circle doesn't get it, find people who do — online LGBTQ+ survivor forums, books, queer trauma support groups, even podcasts or social media creators. Feeling seen will reduce the pressure to prove anything.

Shift the Focus from Explaining to Reclaiming:

Instead of answering the question "Why didn't you leave?" ask yourself: "What am I building, now that I've left — or I'm about to?" Let's keep our energy there, going forward, not backward.

## ◎ KEY TAKEAWAYS

☆ When people ask *"Why didn't you just leave?"* it's a sign of their ignorance and a world that doesn't understand emotional abuse.

☆ Emotional abuse cuts deep, and you are allowed to cry without a visible wound.

☆ You stayed because of trauma bonds, hope, and being trained to doubt yourself, not because you wanted to.

☆ You don't owe anyone an explanation or your story for their comfort.

☆ You can create a "Go-To Response" for doubters that is short, neutral, and final, such as *"Things got difficult."*

**Join me on the other side!**

www.thesparkletrap.com/qr6

# A TRIP TO A NEW "ME"

"Really, I tried to get off the roller coaster multiple times...
Somehow, I thought I was going somewhere.
I didn't realize that I was trapped in a looping circuit.
And when I thought I was somewhere new,
it was the roller coaster that had moved...
but I was still in the car.

I know some people jump...
I waited for that little stop
to get off and finally start really moving.

And walking at first, and on a Rivian later on.
I got on the right track.
I was on
*A Trip to a New Me*"

# CHAPTER 20

# THE PART THAT LET THEM IN

There's a moment, after the storm, when silence sets in.

No more chaos. No more games. No more begging for crumbs.

Just you… and maybe the aching question:

*"Why did I let them in?"*

Not in a shameful way but in a quiet, curious, soul-whispering way. Because while you were surviving, you didn't have the luxury of asking that. But now… now you're safe enough to turn inward.

## IT WAS WOUNDING…

You let them in because they knew how to touch your tender self, the part of you that wanted to fully connect with someone special, the part that was taught that love had to be earned, chased, or fixed. We all carry wounds from childhood, culture, past relationships. And narcissists? They sniff those wounds out like blood in water. They mirror your needs. They perform as the solution. But they never truly see you. They only see what they can extract.

## SELF-BLAME IS A TRAP

Be careful not to weaponize healing. It's easy to go from *"I didn't deserve this"* to *"I must have attracted it."*

From *"I was manipulated"* to *"Maybe I created this."* Or, *"I have to forgive myself for…"*

**No, darling.**

The universe is not attracting the toxic partners in your life. Your nervous system is. Let's use our energy and the universe to attract beautiful things, not to punish ourselves (more).

## HEALING ISN'T A GLOW-UP

Healing isn't about turning your pain into a perfect Instagram arc. It's about sitting with the younger version of you, the one who said yes when they should've said no, the one who kept forgiving, the one who silenced their gut, and saying:

**"You didn't fail me. You were doing your best with what you knew."**

You don't have to go back to your old self in order to heal. You are now moving forward to a new, better version of yourself, one who understands that you are, and always were, enough.

## THE SHAME THAT LINGERS

There's often a hidden shame in realizing you saw red flags and stayed, that you excused things, that you missed things.

But let's be real: survivors are not trained interrogators. We are lovers. Believers. Hope-holders.

And that's not something to be ashamed of. **It's something to protect going forward.**

As I said before in this book, you didn't choose to stay or tolerate. Your wounds and your nervous system did.

# ♛ ACTION STEPS

### Write a Letter to the Version of You Who Let Them In

Not to scold, but to hold. What were they missing? What did they need? What were they hoping for? Let them speak. Then answer with love.

........................................... ....................................................

........................................... ....................................................

....................................................................................................

....................................................................................................

....................................................................................................

### Name the Old Wound / Belief

Maybe it was abandonment. Maybe it was needing to prove your worth. Maybe it was growing up unseen. Naming it helps take its power away

....................................................................................................

....................................................................................................

....................................................................................................

....................................................................................................

....................................................................................................

### Rewire the Wound / Belief

Take the old wound or belief — for example: *"Love means sacrificing myself"* — and rewrite it: *"Love feels safe. I don't have to shrink to be loved."* Repeat it. Post it. Breathe it.

..............................................................................................

..............................................................................................

..............................................................................................

..............................................................................................

..............................................................................................

### Reparent the Ache

When those old feelings come up — neediness, panic, longing — pause. Close your eyes and picture your younger self. Say: *"I've got you now. We're safe."* Then give them what they needed: comfort, validation, permission to walk away.

### Celebrate the Boundaries You Now Hold

Every time you say no, walk away, pause before reacting, or check in with your gut — celebrate it. That's not just healing. That's becoming your own protector.

## ◎ KEY TAKEAWAYS

✫ You let them in because they mirrored your wounds and longings, not because you were weak.

✫ Self-blame only repeats the abuse; compassion breaks the loop.

✫ Healing is not a glow-up — it's an act of re-parenting and self-protection.

✫ The shame of staying too long belongs to the wound, not to your worth.

✫ Rewriting old beliefs ("I must earn love" → "I am lovable as I am") rewires your nervous system toward safety.

✫ Every boundary you hold is proof that the part of you who once said yes when they meant no… is finally safe, loved, and home.

# CHAPTER 21

# THE CONTROVERSY OF FORGIVENESS

The world is constantly telling us that the key to healing is either to "forget and forgive," or, at minimum, to "not forget **but forgive.**"

*Excuse me? Can somebody tell me HTF to do that??*

## UNFORGETTABLE AND UNFORGIVABLE

How many experiences in life have we had that became unforgettable? How many more are yet to come? Hundreds or thousands... Can you choose which one to forget? As if you could just press a delete button in your mind and, poof! *"You're good!"* But you can't, right? Forgetfulness happens over time, and sometimes, it never does.

In general, our brain tends to forget things that are less relevant, less painful, less joyful... Let's say, things in the "Standard" category. But it keeps forever what's been repeated, what impacted us, what felt deeply meaningful.

So why should forgiving be any different? Even when we accept apologies out loud, we're often just forgiving socially, not emotionally.

That doesn't mean the hurt disappears. It doesn't mean the healing process is done.

What if forgiving and forgetting operate on the same neurological system?

As there are unforgettable things, there are also unforgivable things...things out of the "Standard" category. But the fact of "not forgiving" often puts pressure on us. When we don't forgive, people look at us like we're cold, bitter, unspiritual. Like there's something wrong with us.

There are moments when we have to try to drop our cultural baggage and think... how?... thinking **objectively**:

- Would/Should you really forgive someone who is capable of hurting you on purpose?

- Would/Should you really forgive someone who has actively manipulated you for years? (Or long enough to hurt you)

- Would/Should you forgive someone who will help you heal, just to be able to break you afterwards?

- Would/Should you forgive an abuser? I don't know about yours, but my mind says NO.

Think about it this way: If someone comes into your home and destroys it on purpose, would you forgive that? Why would you forgive someone who, on purpose, broke your heart, your nervous system, and your own sense of identity?

Forgiveness can sometimes feel like erasing what happened, like wiping away the responsibility of someone who should be held accountable.

## BUT SOMEONE NEEDS TO BE FORGIVEN!!

And here it comes… the slap in the face that many of us receive, either from our own mind or from the world:

*"You have to forgive yourself."*

Boom! Guilt located… YOU!

*"Because you tolerated…"*
*"Because you stayed…"*
*"Because you chose to do that…"*

**Bullshit.** Yes, I said it. Bullshit.

Because I didn't choose to tolerate, to stay, or to do. My mind, inside of a cycle of abuse and manipulation, did. The wound is choosing, not us.

Forgive yourself for the bad things that you did in your life, but be very careful with the pressure of forgiveness pushing you toward self-blame.

## WHAT IF THERE'S "NOTHING TO FORGIVE"?

Let me be very clear: **in an abusive relationship, the only guilty one is the abuser. Period.**

You don't have to forgive yourself, and you don't have to forgive an abuser in order to heal. Maybe there's nothing to forgive in order to heal, but firmly, deep inside, **locate the blame in the right place.** And when I talk about blaming, I don't mean being angry, getting revenge, punishing… No. I'm talking about accepting that it wasn't our fault. It was PS's fault. And you know what? **Objectively**, it is what it is...

This action can relieve us of that cultural pressure of needing to forgive.

## BLAME AS A BOUNDARY

One day I told myself, *"Let me blame in peace...!"*

Blame in peace means anchoring the truth of what happened, not carrying the burden of anger, but simply letting the shame fall where it belongs. The anger, the rage, the regrets... with time and self-work, they fade. But the gates of your life? They should stay closed to people like this. And maybe blame is one of the vaults where you keep the keys. Think about this:

How many times in your relationship with PS have you forgiven? And what happened after doing so? Did you fall into the trap again? Did you receive another slap?

What if the fact of not forgiving but, instead, properly locating the blame, is containing your new boundaries?

**Note:** If forgiveness brings you peace, beautiful. There are great resources out there to help you with the process, and I encourage you. But if it feels like spiritual pressure or emotional bypassing, you're not alone. There's another way.

# ♛ ACTION STEPS

Straightforward, sweetie... simple: Do you forgive PS?

......................................................................................................

Do you want to forgive, or do you feel social pressure about forgiving?

......................................................................................................

......................................................................................................

......................................................................................................

I want you to take a while to think about this and process without judgment. Journal, take a walk, reflect a little bit... and whenever you're ready, I'm here to continue with you

......................................................................................................

......................................................................................................

......................................................................................................

## 🎯 KEY TAKEAWAYS

★ You don't need to "forget and forgive" to heal; some things are unforgettable and unforgivable.

★ Forgiveness can feel like pressure and can erase the accountability of the abuser.

★ In an abusive relationship, the only person to blame is the abuser, and it's not your fault for **having tolerated it or staying.**

★ Properly placing the blame on the abuser can be an act of setting boundaries and keeping the gates of your life closed to people like that.

★ If forgiveness brings you peace, it is a beautiful path — but if it feels like emotional bypassing, there are other ways to heal.

# CHAPTER 22

# HEALING FROM SOCIAL VALIDATION

It feels great when people tell us, *"You're right!"* It would be great to hear that always, right? It gives us social validation. And most of us are wired to need it.

Our primitive brain is still working... (It seems that evolving doesn't mean deleting the last update and installing a new one!) And there was a time when staying connected meant surviving. It was essential to stay connected and avoid judgment and rejection. If you got kicked out of your tribe, you would die crossing the jungle by yourself. That is still true, even though now "there's no jungle to cross." If you get rejected, you go home, even though it feels terrible, because for the brain, judgment and rejection are big red alerts.

Let me tell you this: Your real healing is in your own hands, not in someone else's. For example:

A therapist will help you find your own breakthroughs, and through them, you will heal.

A person who doesn't understand the depth of abuse can potentially say something harmful to you. (Remember, don't get angry, my sweetie pie.) Why? Because that person is not saying, *"You're right,"* and that feels like judgment or rejection.

It's normal, and many times necessary, to express your feelings with your community. If feeling rejection happens often, you might start feeling disconnected, more confused, and get hurt. This is a healing journey. The gaslighting should be over once you separate.

Even though it feels great (and it can be very healing) to get the people around you to understand you, we don't need it in order to heal. It doesn't mean keeping it as a secret, but choosing better, not casting pearls before swine, and ultimately, deeply knowing your truth. What you have lived and what you have learned are yours. And you don't need anybody to say, "You're right!" in order to heal. So what could we do?

## UNDERSTANDING

Like Froggie in the earlier chapters, you have gone through a complex slow-cooking process. The depth of emotional abuse is big and hard to understand, even for us! At this moment, you are trying to understand something that the world is not ready for — yet.

When you rely on talking to people in order to get understanding (and validation) for something like "I have financial problems," many people will be able to give you ideas or to point out what is failing. This is not like that, but now you are on the right track.

This process touches core values, insecurities, wounds, your own neuro-plasticity, and you need to understand what happened. Find resources (hopefully like this book) that give you a real understanding of the processes happening inside of you: a therapist, books, YouTube channels, trauma experts... Getting to your own understanding is a real healing experience that happens as you find the right resources.

## ACCEPTING

One of the hardest things for me to ground in my own truth was to deeply accept that yes, I was a victim. And once I left, a survivor of abuse. Period.

It took time, actually, in my case. It wasn't until I *kind of* accepted it that I could leave. (It is not the same for everyone!) After I left, the process continued (and I think it still does). To stop judging myself and start accepting that it wasn't my fault took a while. Relaxing and accepting that not everybody is the same took a while…! But each one of those moments where I got to that step of accepting one more thing brought me so much healing!

And it was a process, and probably I'm still in it. It can take time, and that's okay! It is normal! Manipulation and emotional abuse are a thin and delicate line… Reality gets blurred. Our confidence gets damaged… And now we need to start rewiring our minds to get stronger, savvier, more confident, happier, and, as a consequence, sexier! (Don't go to the gym and become a muscle-person "as revenge," please…)

## A NEW CHOSEN FAMILY

Like I said, we are wired to stay connected, and we should, so let's take a look at some possible "right fits."

People who love you for real and will make an effort to understand you and hold your hand are a better choice. Those people may need your time, and it will be worth it to explain your feelings, as they are in "listening mode" instead of "ready-to-judge mode." They might fail, and that's normal! Be patient. It can feel like screaming at the representative of your phone carrier, but they can actually help you…

If you are trying to get help from them, be patient and don't expect people to be in your head. It's a process that will give you support, understanding, and love.

People who have gone through something similar can give you good support. I remember the first time I talked to somebody who had had a relationship with a PS in the past. They also needed to gain resources in order to understand what was going on and to leave. My whole system felt like, "Finally!!" and it was very freeing and healing. Talking to each other, we got to understand missing pieces of our own puzzles.

There are many ways to connect with a whole great community of people going through the healing process, inspiring others after recovery, creating beautiful things… And you are getting there too, my love.

Professionals with training in abuse are an excellent resource for you. A therapist or a trauma-related coach (depending on your needs) can be a great ally during the process. There are specialized LGBTQ+ organizations too… Please, we have gold in our community!

Acting on the advice in this chapter doesn't mean discarding people (although sometimes in life we should). It means creating a community to count on, to talk with freely, and also, when you are ready, to hold someone else's hand.

We are not alone, my dear!

# ♕ ACTION STEPS

List below the people who make you feel understood, safe, and loved. This could be a friend, a family member, a therapist, or even a book or a podcast. Next to each name, write down why they are a safe space for you. The goal is to visually see the support you already have and to consciously seek out more of it. You are building your new chosen family.

..............................................................................................

..............................................................................................

..............................................................................................

..............................................................................................

..............................................................................................

..............................................................................................

..............................................................................................

..............................................................................................

..............................................................................................

..............................................................................................

..............................................................................................

..............................................................................................

## ◎ KEY TAKEAWAYS

★ You don't need social validation from others to heal, even though it can feel good.

★ Your primitive brain is still wired to fear rejection because, historically, it meant being kicked out of your tribe and dying alone.

★ Healing comes from gaining your own understanding of the complex abuse you experienced, accepting it, and creating a new community of people who support you.

★ You can find resources and connect with a community of survivors who understand your experience, which is a freeing and healing experience.

★ Accepting that you were a victim and are now a survivor is a process, but it is necessary to move forward and stop judging yourself.

# CHAPTER 23

# THE HAIR ON MY EARS

*"Once upon a time, I was gifted with a beard... but to receive that gift, I had to pay a price...*

*Hair on my ears!!"*

I don't know how many times in my life those hairs have been waxed... and I also don't know how many times I forgot and wore them, being unaware... until somebody made a joke.

Darling, they grow very fast... Also, it's about genetics... I didn't choose to have them!

One day, I just didn't care anymore. I decided to accept them. Sometimes wax comes into play, many other times it doesn't... I just don't fight against them anymore. But wait, I don't do "resigning." I actually went through truly accepting that they are part of my body, and on the "Scale of Disaster," they are insignificant.

This chapter is about accepting, not about being resigned, which sometimes can give us a false sense of "acceptance," but is not the same.

Resigning comes from surrendering to a fact, event, experience, or thought because of a lack of control over it. Once you see you cannot control it, you can either go or surrender. This is where the "Fuck It Energy" comes into place, emotional, exhausted, but still there. Trying to be okay with unacceptable things by resigning.

Accepting, on the other hand, comes from a different point of view. Let's use a "Grindr-type" example:

**Profile Name:** XL [+eggplant emoji]. When you fully accept something, you don't hide it. You make it part of your nature. If it brings you confidence (like the add-on "XL"), then the better you feel about it, the more you want to play with it… (LOL).

Now a more generic example:

Imagine that you feel comfortable with most of your body, but you don't like your toenails. What would you do? Do you hide them or shit-talk about them from "false acceptance"? While on the days you don't wear flip-flops, your body simply flows…

Do you get it? The vibe and your feelings are different.

> [You] *Daniel… where are we going with this?*

Healing requires different things… and I summarize them this way: admitting, accepting, rewiring.

Like "new parts" of our body, now we have new parts working in our mind and nervous system. With a big difference: I cannot make my body stop growing hairs on my ears (yes, I already tried laser…), but I can change my mind and the way my nervous system operates. It is called **neuro-plasticity.**

How can I change from triggered to healed?

## THE POSSIBLE "NEW HAIRS"

This section should never keep you in the role of victim. We were victims while the relationship lasted; the moment we leave, we are survivors. Wounds heal at their own pace with the right attention. But not everything is a wound. We also gained muscle, so in the Action Steps I'll propose that you make a list (template down

197

there), and I want you to write down all the new parts that you can find as a consequence of your experience with PS.

In my case, I admitted that I'm way braver about fighting for myself. My confidence was very damaged, but now I prioritize myself more. The exposure to the queer sex life was triggering, and I had "new trust issues." A part of me was still judging myself, and now I was way more aware and sensitive to "subtexts."

I went through admitting as much as I could. For me, to see some of the journal entries was painful, so let's look at it like a doctor exploring our body after crashing the bike, or like financial planning. You can't control your money if you don't know your expenses/income, right? Let's go through this… objectively… *yes!* Remember, some of those new parts of you are strengths, so list them too!

## UNDERSTANDING IS POWER

We have "new parts" in our system, and admitting that we have them is key to starting to really understand, deep inside, what those new behaviors or feelings mean.
We cannot change what we don't understand. But once we are checking our "emotional body," we can detect the parts that need some attention. With resources (books, good YouTube videos, a nurturing community, a therapist…) and, very importantly, self-reflection, we are creating the perfect environment for positive change.

In this phase, we will also understand what role those new parts have in our mind. You will find that some new parts of you are actually good; some others cause pain; and some are simply facts.

So when we look at the list of things we admitted as new parts, we'll go through the process of evaluating them one by one:

- I feel way more brave to fight for myself → Is this good? Let's work toward acceptance.

- I have been a victim of abuse → Fact. Let's work toward acceptance of it as a fact and work on the damage produced as a consequence.

- I have trust issues that make it harder to connect → Let's work toward deeper understanding and rewiring that.

**Note:** Please, work on the parts that you can recognize as painful. Healing is possible. Over time, if we hold onto pain without processing it, it can morph into something that keeps us stuck. Let's stay compassionate with ourselves while also moving toward healing.


## THE THREE WAYS WE CHANGE

Keeping it simple, our "New Update" can happen in three different ways:

**Immediately – Cumulatively – Retroactively**

**Immediately:** Something impactful can create immediate change in your behavior. Like a traumatic event changes us, a breakthrough can change us too. During the process of understanding, you may experience breakthroughs that will heal and change you immediately. That will also make you create new boundaries or take some kind of action (not revenge!!) that will lead you toward healing. At that very moment, your behavior, at some level, will change.

**Cumulatively:** One of the ways the mind learns is through repetition. But this time, let's use it to our advantage. Repeating affirmations or listening to a self-hypnosis audio for 21 days or more will filter from your conscious mind, where we have to do things "by effort," to be retained by your subconscious mind, where it starts becoming part of you.

**Retroactively:** This has more to do with the awareness of change. Meaning, sometimes we have changed, but we don't notice it until afterward. For example, the day you have a new partner and you don't get a reply to your text — and suddenly you notice that it didn't trigger your insecurity. "Byeee!"

Without the proper context, this might sound quite simplistic, and I'm not trying to say that healing is simple. But please, don't underestimate the power of this tool and think about this specifically.

We cannot self-generate immediate change by ourselves, like crafting a breakthrough, but we can expose ourselves to resources that can lead to them. We cannot be aware of retroactive change until one day we are, but we can still do our "reps," and one day we'll notice the change. What we can do, though, is to use cumulative change. I'll drop some help in the Action Steps section of this chapter.

The combination of all these elements compounds the process of healing. It is a journey, and sometimes it feels uncomfortable, but that one day you look back and feel empowered will make it worthwhile.

# ♛ ACTION STEPS

Let's take a personal inventory. Create three columns in a notebook.

—  In the first column, list the "New Parts" you've noticed about yourself (e.g., *trust issues, more sensitive to subtexts*).

—  In the second column, label them as either a *Strength*, a *Wound*, or a *Fact*.

—  In the third column, write one sentence about how you feel about it.

This is not about judgment; it's about seeing yourself objectively, as a survivor — as the shiny and radiant beauty of nature that you are, even with some wounds, my love.

## ⦿ KEY TAKEAWAYS

★ This chapter uses the metaphor of hair on the ears to talk about accepting new parts of yourself that have developed as a result of the abuse — both good and painful.

★ It distinguishes between *resigning* to something out of a lack of control and *accepting* it and learning to live with it confidently.

★ Healing involves three processes: admitting what happened, accepting it, and "rewiring" your mind and nervous system through neuro-plasticity.

★ You can see change in three ways: immediately (through breakthroughs), cumulatively (through repetition of affirmations), and retroactively (when you notice a change has already happened).

★ The goal is to admit the "new parts" of yourself objectively, work on the painful ones, and use repetition to move toward a more positive mindset.

# CHAPTER 24

# COMPASSION... AND SELF-COMPASSION!

My dear... my love... what a journey, eh? So many feelings, and so raw...

It is normal that sometimes we feel waves of rage, vengefulness, repulsion... It is normal to judge yourself from time to time.

It is normal that sometimes we go deeper into a terrible self-dialogue. I've been there too. In those moments, we need to go to compassion. And do you know where it is? In your self-love. There.

I want to guide you through one of my favorite exercises to find the roadmap that leads to compassion.

I want you to think for a second about those bad things you say to yourself. Find the most recurrent ones... "I'm a disaster, a mess, stupid, a failure..."

Take a minute, sweetie. **Think**.

Now that you have a list, hopefully it's a small one (that maybe repeats too often), think about this:

If a roommate, a partner, a peer at work, or even your boss said those same sentences to you... would you tolerate it?

**If not... why do you tolerate it from yourself?**

Self-shit-talk is one of the fastest ways to depression. We have to get out of that.

Take those three main sentences... or four.

I'm not going to tell you, "Write the opposite! and bury your shit!" Don't worry.

The key is to go from **super-negative** to **harmless-negative**. Your brain is not stupid and it won't believe the opposite of something you say to yourself so often. But it will accept something that at least has the same negative root.

This sounds something like this:

From *"Stupid piece of shit"* to... *"Little glitter-fart of the universe."*

[You] *Wait, what?*

Yeah... I know it's shocking, but I'm asking you to do it for a reason.

We are going to take our worst phrases and create something that, although negative like "fart," very importantly... will make us laugh.

Come on, darling, give it a try. Get creative!

Every time your mind goes to those old sentences (the terrible ones) and you catch yourself, say those new sentences! All the bad feelings produced by your brain assuming that what you are saying is true (you know it is not, that's why you wouldn't tolerate it! But your brain doesn't care!) **vanish**. Stay in those new sentences for a little bit. Repeat them, and don't let the bad ones come in.

And remember: hug yourself, say "It's okay...," "We are safe," "I got you now."

Now, it is normal that you tend to get angry every time somebody gets along with PS... *"They believe their version!"* (That's our head talking).

They are somewhere on the way to being victims... victims of being manipulated, of getting hooked, of believing the wrong version.

The picture you are seeing of PS with another person?

Look at the eyes of that new person. Look at the smile.

Send that person the strength you know is needed. Send that person love. Send that person an ethereal message:

**You will smile back, my love.**

And that's it. Don't be angry, my love. Always think from compassion... the compassion you were denied many times.

# ♛ ACTION STEPS

Did you do it...? Sweetie...?

**Sweetie-Forms™**

Did you say something nice to yourself today?

Yes? No? .............................................

Can you say right now: I'm enough, I'm enough, I'm enough? You don't need to shout it, my dear.

And... did you do it?

Yes? No? .............................................

## ◎ KEY TAKEAWAYS

☆ In moments of rage, self-judgment, or terrible self-talk, you need to turn to compassion and self-love.

☆ You can challenge negative self-talk by creating "harmless-negative" phrases that make you laugh, helping your brain accept a gentler inner dialogue.

☆ You should not tolerate verbal abuse from yourself, just as you wouldn't tolerate it from a partner, roommate, or boss.

☆ When you see the narcissist with a new person, instead of getting angry, you can think from a place of compassion, recognizing that the new person is also on a journey to becoming a victim.

☆ The goal is to let go of anger and think with compassion, sending love and strength to the new person in the narcissist's life.

# CHAPTER 25

# YOU ARE RADIANT

Once upon a time, you were afraid to take up space.

You learned to whisper instead of speak, to ask nicely instead of demand, to dim your sparkle because someone told you it was "too much."

You twisted your truth into smaller pieces so it could fit inside someone else's comfort zone instead of making them choke.

While they were on their phone, you begged for love, and then you were punished for needing it.

**But look at you now.**

You cried, screamed internally, nodded too hard, maybe even laughed with one of those snorts that only happen when something truly hits. You remembered things you had tried to forget, but you also saw yourself more clearly than you ever have.

Let me tell you something you need to hear, darling radiant loving creature, not as a technique, or a mantra, or a cognitive reframe. Just as plain truth:

*Even in the fog.*
*Even in the confusion.*

**You were brilliant.**

I know you might still feel fragile, as if healing were a performance you were not doing right.
Let me say this loud, my love:

*Healing isn't a glittery epiphany in a yoga retreat.*
*It's texting your bestie instead of them.*
*It's journaling instead of "spiralizing."*
*Not explaining. Not reacting.*
*It's sleeping through the night for the first time in weeks.*
*It's remembering that **you are the center of your own story now.***

*Not a side character.*
*Not a savior.*
*Not a mirror.*
*Not a punching bag dressed as a partner.*
***Not a joke.***

***After being in hell, now you're designing your heaven.***

And I don't mean that in a woo-woo way (though if you wanna burn sage and scream "I'm a bad bitch!" into the ocean, I fully support it).

I mean: you are now equipped with truth, tools, and boundaries… even superpowers!

**That's sacred.**

*You are radiant not because they couldn't destroy you,*

**but because you rebuilt yourself without needing them.**

So here's your final glitter-chant. Say it out loud, whisper it in bed, scream it from your chest. Whatever you do, mean it:

*I am not what they did to me.*
*I am what I choose to become now.*
*I am radiant, fierce, whole, and finally mine.*
*I am... unapologetically radiant.*

**[Emoji sunglasses]**
**[Emoji rainbow]**
**[Emoji rocket]**
**[Emoji nails]**
**[And emoji disco ball]**

**[You]** *OMG Froggie?*
**[Me]** *Holy cow, did you take steroids?*
**[Froggie]** *Hi Sweeties! No... I just had to train hard in order to jump out of the pot.*
*I saw it so clearly... I fell in the trap of a perverse narcissist but I could finally see it... and here I am.*
*Freer, wilder, wiser, stronger, sexier, sassier...*
*And as I move forward, my burns are healing.*

# 👑 FINAL ACTION

Write your own closing line. Seriously. Right now.

No journaling rules. No grammar police. No expectations.

Just... what do you want to say to yourself at the end of this story?

Here's a prompt if you need it:

*Today, I leave this chapter knowing...*

*And from now on, I will...*

(Go ahead, sparkle-sweetie-writer. The pen is yours.)

........................................................................................................

........................................................................................................

........................................................................................................

........................................................................................................

........................................................................................................

*When you're ready, close this book.*

*Breathe.*

*Look in the mirror.*

*Smile, even if it's wobbly.*

*Then go live your beautiful life.*

*And if someday you forget your power, come back.*

*This chapter will be here, waiting for you... but not expecting you.*

**I love you.**

##  KEY TAKEAWAYS

★ You are a "radiant, fierce, whole" person who was brilliant even in the fog and confusion of the abusive relationship.

★ Healing is a messy, everyday process that involves small, intentional acts like texting a best friend instead of the abuser.

★ You are the center of your own story now — no longer a side character, a savior, or a punching bag.

★ You are equipped with new tools, truth, and boundaries.

★ You are radiant not because they couldn't destroy you, but because you rebuilt yourself without needing them.

**Meet me on the other side!**

www.thesparkletrap.com/qr7

# BONUS CHAPTERS

# CHAPTER 26

# "THAT NEW PERSON" — BONUS CHAPTER

In this bonus chapter, we are going to explore two different sides of "that new person."

Their new person, and your new person.

Both can be deeply moving chapters in your life after breaking up with a PS.

Let's break it down:

## THEIR NEW PERSON

As we said before… **compassion!**

You are so, so, *so* blessed that the picture you saw doesn't contain your image! **Congratulations!**

**Don't be tempted. Don't interfere.**

Don't put yourself in their sights again. Keep going with your life!

But if you still find it difficult to feel compassion for that person, let me tell you a real story… with some little tweaks for privacy.

*Pedro was from Italy. He was the boyfriend of someone from Oakland, let's call him David.*

*During their long relationship, David always wanted to move to Italy, start a business there, and build a nice life together. They would joke about the possibility of getting married so David could get a visa and about the fact that **Pedro was still married to his ex…***

*One day, after eleven years of a roller-coaster relationship, things exploded, and they broke up.*

*The next month, Instagram was flooded with pictures of Pedro with a new person: a cute, young guy from Italy visiting California. He got hooked…*

*So hooked that after two months, suddenly they were in… a famous city in Oklahoma… to get married!*

*Can you imagine how David felt?*

*The message was brutal: After eleven years, you didn't get this, but someone I just met did.*

*But suddenly, the Instagram flood stopped. What happened?*

*They couldn't get married…*

***Because Pedro was already married!***

*WTF!?*

Next thing, the boy just got kicked to the curb after that.

Can you imagine the poor guy? Thinking he was going to change his life and move to the U.S.?

Getting ready to marry a new, intense lover… someone so shiny that he was blinded for a while…

Used just for someone to send a message.

And that is how narcissists use people, just a little bit or a lot. They don't care.

Once, you were there too… it just lasted longer.

**Compassion.**

## YOUR NEW PERSON

Okay, you've met someone else. Exciting!

It can be a great sign for you. Things are going well!

But let's go a little deeper, okay?

You've processed so much. You feel stronger. And now... you have a new partner. Yay!

What could go wrong?

**The reactivation of triggers you thought were gone. That's it.**

Later, we'll see what to do with them, but for now, let's keep exploring.

Did you know that in your relationship with PS, there were *"special triggering situations"*?

Yes, right? Have you been exposed to them since? ...Nope!

That's why now it's possible that you'll find a section of your heart that didn't really heal, because it didn't need to.

But now, the *Detective Mode* is turning on again... WTF is happening!?

That first time you and your partner have to stay apart, with a bunch of miles in between.

The first time your partner goes out for one night — or for a whole weekend — and you're not there.

You name it. That sudden and first triggering moment that's coming from someone else.

The first thing I want you to ask yourself is:

**"Am I again... with a PS?"**

[You] *Wow!! What?*

Pay attention, sweetie. **We are magnets for narcissists.**

If you've fallen into the trap again, the beginning will look like someone who fits your entire system.

**They are mimicking you.**

Look back, please. Any red flags?
Any moment of gaslighting?
Any signs of devaluation?
Anything your brilliant mind chose to bypass…?
  Sweetie? Let's stay sharp, okay?
  Look at it. Be raw and real with yourself.

Analyze:

- I asked for something important to me… did it happen?

- Did you notice "wishy-washy" sharing of information?

- Did you feel you were being labeled as reactive or controlling?

- Did you provide resources to this person, like books or videos, to improve your relationship? Were they read… or ignored?

Pay attention.
  Now, reply to the question without judging yourself:

**"Am I again… with a PS?"**

If the answer is **Yes**…

Someone up there… bless them.
  Because do you know what?

This game isn't new for you. But for them, dealing with someone who has the right tools, even superpowers,

**is new.**

When this happens, because someone dares to manipulate a survivor of narcissistic abuse, your feelings of anger and guilt may come rushing back.

It's okay, darling. There's a lot we can learn from here.

**Judging OFF - Compassion ON**

You have multiple tools now. It's time to reopen your…

**Narci-Box™**

This new relationship can really show you areas to heal, repeating patterns, open wounds…

Let's focus on *leaving*, not on *self-judging*, okay, sweetie?

If the answer is **No…**

It's possible you've just experienced some triggering moments. So, communicate, my love. If you are with a good person, communication is key.

It won't go against you. It's safe, even if you're still scared of sharing.

Share your triggers. Work on them with your loving new person. Keep growing…

But never forget:

**You are the number one on your own VIP list.**

# ♕ ACTION STEPS

Was it a **yes?** Are you with a new PS?

I'm very sorry, but always remember:

**we got this.**

Go to the Hidden Chapters. There we analyze the moment when the first love-bombing stage starts to crumble.

**Refresh your superpowers.**

Was it a **no?**

OMG, I'm so happy for you!

In this case, I recommend the book *Attached*, by Amir Levine and Rachel S. F. Heller.

Give it to your new partner too, it can help you go in the right direction.

**See you on the other side – one more time!**

www.thesparkletrap.com/qr8

## ⊚ KEY TAKEAWAYS

☆ Seeing the narcissist with a new person can be very emotional, but you should not be tempted to interfere.

☆ The new person is likely a new victim who is also being used, as illustrated by the story of "Pedro," "David," and the young Spanish guy.

☆ Meeting a new person after a breakup can be a great sign, but it can also reactivate old triggers you thought were gone.

☆ You need to stay vigilant and ask yourself if you are falling into a new "trap" with another narcissist.

☆ It's important to analyze a new relationship for red flags and to be raw and real with yourself, not bypassing signs of devaluation or gaslighting.

☆ When you are with a good person, communicate. But never forget — you are the main character of your life.

# CHAPTER 27

# LET IT GO, HON
# – BONUS CHAPTER

*One day I knew I was right.*
*I was hurt.*
*I prepared to go.*

*I was right.*

*Someone I loved manipulated me.*

*I knew I was right!*

*I was ready to take it to the end.*

*I knew I was right…*

*And suddenly, a voice popped into my head:*

*"When life shifts, it's tempting to sink into the shadows.*
*Clutching pain too tightly leaves no hand free for the light.*
*Reaching for that light can feel impossible,*
*until you decide to let go."*

*It felt as if my heart was suddenly melting.*

*All my emotional defenses were still working.* **Hacker Mode ON.**

*Anticipating betrayal. Scanning for traps.*

*Not because I was still in danger…*

*But because I was still carrying the weight of pain.*

*Pain was like another part of me.*

*And now I see it.*

*And I can work to let it go.*

*Let me gift you with one last tool in this book…*

## THE HEALING METER™

*In our own reactions, we can find what I call the Healing Meter™.*
When you feel your body rushing, think:

*What is hurting? Why?*
*What made me react this way?*
*Observe your reactions in order to heal.*

*And even if someone* **dares** *to manipulate someone as well-equipped as you…*
**let's be fair with our reactions.**

*Let's not judge. Let's not weaponize our expertise.*

*We live in a world where we all can manipulate,*
*but not everyone is a narcissist.*

*We all lie sometimes…*
*and it never feels nice to find out a hidden truth.*

*But let's not give more power to our past.*
*Let's stop that past from blurring our minds,*
*just because our sensors now work too well.*

*Simply breathe, wait, and see.*
*Don't judge too quickly, baby.*

*And always remember…*

*If we need to…*
*now we know how to play it even better than a narcissist, right?*

**[Chuckles]**

*You have proven to be strong,*
*you needed to.*

*Now, keep your power.*
*Let go of your pain.*
*Boost the sparkle and…*
*…breathe.*

# ♛ ACTION STEPS

Breathe deeply three times. Or more.

Take just a few seconds to breathe it, to smile in the meantime…

It's a micro-ritual.

Do it every day, it's like botox for your heart.

## ◎ KEY TAKEAWAYS

★ Holding on to pain, rage, and betrayal from the past prevents you from "grabbing the light" and moving forward.

★ Stop letting the past blur your mind just because your new sensors for manipulation are working so well.

★ You have proven to be strong and gained the power to handle difficult situations.

★ The key is to keep your power but let go of the pain.

# THE END

**To my biggest love: Max...**

*In my darkest moments you were my light.*
*Six years in my life and you rescued me,*
*changed me.*
*You gave me a north star.*

*You left too soon, though... fuck.*
*I really wish you were here right now,*
*but I think somehow you're giving me the strength*
*to look back,*
*to look inside,*
*and to transform my deepest wounds*
*into something so special.*

*I miss you,*
*I love you,*
*Every day I look up and send you a kiss.*

*Daniel*

# SPECIAL THANKS TO...

*"...I'll eternally be grateful for you, California, for giving me the perfect environment to create what I hope will be a helpful tool for my beloved LGBTQ+ Community."*

*"You took a trailer and got to downtown Madrid. Blocking the streets you took me, my things, my motorbike, and helped me escape... I will always remember that day. Thank you so much, your brother"*

*"Lau, Lau, Lau! You crossed the world when I needed you the most...
Thank you,
you really gave me wings"*

*"You supported me even when none of us understood. Even with different opinions, even with my confused perception and your wrong advice... we made it.
Mimi, YoYo
I love you"*

*"G, thank you so much for accepting the challenge of editing this book. I would have never published it without you!"*

# Join the Zero Contact Club Community Today!

www.thesparkletrap.com/community

## Strengthen your support network with this 30 minutes course FOR THEM

Sweetie, I have created a course to share with your friends and family members, maybe you can watch it with someone who is trying to support you.

It is free in the community (#FreeResources section)

www.thesparkletrap.com/support-me-right

**Narci-Thanks™ to "my" abusers:**

www.thesparkletrap.com/narci-thanks

THE PORTAL
TO YOUR
SUPER
POWERS

Disclaimer:

If you are in a volatile situation (physical threats, severe
financial control, etc.), please prioritize escaping and
seeking professional help immediately.
The next three chapters contain real tools to navigate
a relationship with a narcissist,
WHILE YOU GET READY TO GO.
These tools should not be used to continue in an
abusive relationship longer than necessary.
Tools like the Superpower or the Hacker Mode™
are shared to create a controlled "exit strategy" rather than
long-term engagement.

These chapters contain specific tools to *handle*, *spot*, and *emotionally
outmaneuver* a narcissistic abuser.

They've been hidden here, far from the table of contents and the
natural page order, to keep them safe from curious eyes.

Now turn the page.
Welcome to being **Narci-Strategic**™
and welcome to your new toolkit,
the **Narci-Box**™

[Emoji Sunglasses]

# HIDDEN CHAPTER 1

# THE EGGSHELL FLOOR

Those eggshells you have been walking on? They are not eggshells, my love. They are pieces of their mask falling off, while they keep rebuilding it.

Between the Love Bombing phase and Devaluation phase, the first signs of the mess about to come start showing up... You are going to start seeing a lighter version of how the dynamic of your relationship is going to look like from now on.

This part is really upsetting... I know... But the hardest part is to understand what's truly happening...

That you are now living in a wave of **emotional manipulation.**

So! The first thing to understand is: **The real damage is not "the actions they take" behind your suspicions.** It's the fact of **deliberately dragging you into your own insecurities on purpose**, to a land of instability, sadness, to that intense feeling of... *"Why? Why are they doing this?"*

That's the real damage, along with the actions they'll take...!

**Reminder:** Everything behind the "fog" is exactly what they would never tolerate from you. **Those are not only their areas of expansion (and restriction for you) but also the areas containing their own biggest insecurities.**

That's why they will **never** admit the truth.

The second important thing is "**understanding the WTF!**" you are living in, how the trap is working underneath.

Emotional manipulation is not just *gaslighting*... it's a **combination of elements** that will totally confuse you.

Recognizing and understanding combos like these is **totally key** to starting to get some sanity. Let's take a quick overview to see what they look like, but we will explain more in depth in chapter 8 - (Devaluation phase).

Let me gift you with the... *"PS's Bar Classic Combos!!"*:

## 1- Emotional Redirection Daily Combo:

**Accountability Avoidance + Emotional Redirection + Image Management**

The traditional combo for every morning. Instead of saying: **"I did this wrong,"** they say: **"I don't want to do anything that hurts you, and now I know."**

[Us] ??

They bypass naming the action and center your feelings instead, and protect their "caring" persona. *Combo!*

This is used for EVERYTHING in their lives. Admit they left the milk out of the fridge and say it was you, that's the basis. From there, they are **never** accountable, but they sound good...

## 2- "The Wishy-Washy Mode":

**Deliberate Ambiguity + Gaslighting + Emotional Withholding + Emotional Whiplash.**

[Us] *So what are you doing with the guys?*

[PS] *Well, after the party, there are some options,* [silence, texting someone else while talking to you on the phone. Emotional Withholding]

[Long pause…Emotional Withholding]

[Us] *Hello? Are you still there?*

[PS] *Yeah.*

[Us] *So… The plans…?* [You need to push in order to get a normal answer… Controller!]

[PS Angry - Emotional Whiplash] *I don't really know. As soon as I know, don't worry, I will let you know.*

(They won't. But they will manipulate you though…).

Not only do they know that deliberate ambiguity will activate your alerts, but they are also doing this as a way to avoid emotional commitment, so they can provide these answers later:

*I didn't lie, I just hadn't decided… It was just a possibility… You're misinterpreting me again…*

**Closure with the classic: Gaslighting + Blame-shifting.**

**Simply strategic vagueness.**

When they **don't want to be accountable** they blur everything. So, confusion wasn't a side effect… it was the actual goal.

## 3- Preventive Manipulation:

**Gaslighting + Covert Guilt-tripping + Reversal + Blame-shifting
+ Reality Rewriting.**

[Us] *Hon, I think I'm going to go... I'm tired. But you can stay, I'll be
okay. Or if you want, I can stay for a little bit longer...*

[PS] *Well... I would like you to stay, but also... You can't have
a dragonfly as a pet... you can't change people... Dragonflies
need to fly...* **Red Alert: "Dragonfly as the misunderstood
free spirit". Guilt-tripping + Grandiosity + Glamorized
Detachment.**

[Us] *Wait what? I think this doesn't apply to us. Actually, I'm trying
to leave, and give you space... WTF? Why are you saying all this?*
Just you Freaking Out...

[PS] One Hour Monologue (framing you as a something you're
not while you are asking them to stop.)

[Once you are upset...]

[PS] *If you wanna go, I'm okay with that.* (**Then, when finally you
are sad**). *I'd like you to stay.* **Guilt-tripping + Reversal.**

[Next Morning]

[PS] *Hon, what I was trying to say yesterday about the dragonfly,
was actually something beautiful. I think you misunderstood...*
**Gaslighting + Reality Rewriting + Blame-shifting.**

*One day I understood that for you "the dragonfly flying" just meant destroying your nose and/or your asshole MORE... so please, go fly.*

## 4- Social Manipulation - Damage of your Image:

## (More in Chapter 7)

### Gaslighting + Reality Rewriting + Gaslighting...+ + + ...

[PS] *I know this trip might be tough for you, so tell me: what would help you feel calmer while I'm away with my friends?* **Weaponized Empathy**

[Us] *Honestly, just a quick "Goodnight" text would mean a lot. That's all I need.*

[Two days later after disappearing]

[PS – Group video call] *Heyyyyy! Look who's here!* [friends wave at the screen]

[PS] *Oh, by the way, I'll probably be up late again — the team insisted on karaoke.* [friends in background:] *"...and clubs! And drugs!"* **Gaslighting**

[Us] *Wait, you said this was a retreat... what do you mean by "up late again"?*

[PS] *So now I need your permission for when the retreat ends? Do I have to log my bedtime for you?* [coworkers laugh awkwardly] **Reality Rewriting (framing us as controlling in front of others.)**

[Our face freezes into a poker face.]

Of course, the one thing we asked for — that single "Goodnight" text — never came. Because it would've given us real reassurance. And reassurance is the last thing they want us to feel.

**5- "You are too sensitive"… but don't do what I do.**
**[One of PS's favorites!)**

**Emotional Minimization + Blame-shifting.**

> [PS] … *I slept with those three guys yes, but nothing sexual you know… we had a great talk… hanging out…* **Emotional Minimization + Denied Intention.**

> [Us - This question is key] *So, is it okay if I do that too??* **Reaffirmation of Boundaries/Agreements.**

> [PS angry - Emotional Whiplash] *Hey, I'm telling you nothing happened, we are just friends, I like the vibe… You are being paranoid again, seriously… And I guess that you want to sleep with people right? Cos if you are asking me that, it's because you want to!* **Gaslighting + Blame-Shifting.**

> [PS angry] *…You know what? I have to go, we'll talk more…* [hang up] **Narrative Dominance.**

> [Us and our poker face] *But… Is it okay if I do it??*

That's what they will **never** answer, hon…

**They want to expand their freedom and constrict yours.**

As you know, the combos in the devaluation phase feel terrible, but those are just breadcrumbs to keep you on alert, to play with the perception of reality, yours and of the people around them.

These are clear signs that **Discard** is coming. So unless you are already diving deep in this new PhD on *"What the fuck is this person doing?"* or you are not going to be ready...

... when they try to force you to have sex in a car, after both of you getting drunk at a concert and you not feeling ok... **Sexual Coercion.**

...and when you react...

You end up dizzy and emotionally destroyed, walking in the middle of nowhere.

Not allowed in the car, even though you are begging them for help. **Emotional Punishment (for setting up a limit.)**

The answer was NO. **Abandonment as Control.**

Unless... *you apologize because you were "aggressive."* (the moment you reacted saying no to sexual coercion.) **Blame-shifting.**

## THE TRIPLE SLAP

All these Classic Combos are happening around you, pretty much constantly... so unless you are an "Unfortunate Pro" *(Hey there!)* it is hard to detect them at first sight. Hopefully you won't need to deal with them for too much longer...

So, we are starting to see now how there is a game going on. Before, the focus was to find evidence of *"what's behind the fog,"* and *"uncover the double life"* without understanding that the simple fact of living in the fog or feeling your partner has a double life IS THE PROBLEM.

We don't need to focus on finding them at the orgy, or doing that thing they are hiding...

**We need to focus on confirming that we live manipulated, suffering emotional abuse**

Let me simplify something for you to pay attention to:

If your partner is a narcissist, you are living three types of manipulation constantly. It is what I call the *Triple Slap Technique*…

The first one is *"Image Manipulation."* We talked about it in chapter 7, and soon we'll see how they use it to handle the agreements and gain freedom.

The second one is what I call *"Direct Damage."* Here, they will use things like deliberate ambiguity or intermittent reinforcement, until getting to a discard, like disappearing, humiliating you, etc. This Direct Damage is not always obvious, sometimes it is completely unexpected. Here is where we feel the need of checking on PS.

The third one is *"Avoidance Damage"* (formally known as DARVO: Deny, Attack, Reverse Victim and Offender). And here is where you can very easily see clear signs of a bigger picture… After the Direct Damage, they will change strategy to avoid accountability at all costs. They'll use a lot of blame-shifting, future-faking, emotional redirections, emotional whiplash… And there are some questions you might ask that can lead them to use these techniques in exaggerated and obvious ways. This is the time to see the evidence.

In the third Hidden Chapter, you will learn what I call *Narci-Questions*™. They will help you confirm. But for now, stick with me, darling…

## Funnel Agreements

[You:] *Okay, I live in a trap, I get it… but what for??*

[Me:] *They want to do what they want. They do not want you to what you want.*

Picture a funnel turned sideways.

Wide on one side. Narrow on the other. Right? Just in case you didn't realize, you are in the narrow side…

That's what the agreements actually are, behind the fog. Freedom for them; restriction for you.

They get to explore, experiment, disappear for a weekend, go "off the grid"…And you? You get to honor the agreements. You get to hold space. You get to protect their feelings.

Cute, right?

Then they apologize and over time, they do it again… **but not you!**

So, if you take a look at all those "funnel agreements," you start seeing…

### A roadmap of their own insecurities

Think about it! Everything they do, but they wouldn't tolerate your doing. Because it would hurt them, make them feel insecure… **They wouldn't tolerate living with insecurity**, like you do.

And do you know what?

That is great information! Maybe we need to use it along the way…

**The fog is a setup. But once you see it, you're already on your way out.**

Through manipulation tools, they create these Funnel-Agreements. Now, let me introduce you to a simple tactic they also use. I call it the…

## Brag and Accuse

*"Let me hear you brag, and I'll tell you what you lack"*

[Also from the Glossary of Spanish Popular Sayings]

Let me tell you a couple of stories…

I have NEVER in my life introduced myself with the word *"honesty."* I just try to live it. I admit mistakes, I apologize when I mess up, and I do my best to be straightforward. But I've never gone around saying, "I'm the most honest person you'll ever meet."

Do you know who did, though? The one who lied the most. Every introduction, every chat with friends, the word "honesty" appeared like a badge. "You know me, I'm brutally honest!" "With me, it's all honesty!" Non-stop.

And the moment I confronted PS about a clear lie — the first thing out of their mouth? "Everyone knows I'm the most honest person in this room!" (lol, lol, lol).

So… at a dinner table… after twisting stories… you are preaching about honesty? Can somebody pass me the popcorn, please?

And same thing happens with accusations… As Michael James Schneider (IG: @blcksmith) says in one of his artworks:

*"Accusations from a narcissist are actually confessions"*

## Boom…

They will complain, hurt, even cry from something they are accusing you of… **that they do.**

Do you see it? How they use their words to hide and manipulate? The more they talk about something, the more they lack it…

With these types of speeches and the rest of the manipulation tools listed on this book, they manipulate our (and other people's) perception to keep us in the narrow side of the funnel, while they *"thrive"*...

**Special thanks to Michael... Your art gave me strength in the worst moment of my life.**

## 👑 ACTION STEPS

Combo! - Tell me, have you visited PS's Bar? Have you tried any of the Classics? Which one have you seen most frequently?

..............................................................................................................

..............................................................................................................

..............................................................................................................

..............................................................................................................

Let's make a list! Think about all those things PS repeats over and over. Think also about those out-of-the-blue accusations. I'm sure you'll find a few… This way we are going to review our agreements: Are they real, or are they funnels?

..............................................................................................................

..............................................................................................................

..............................................................................................................

..............................................................................................................

Now, let's think about the agreements in the relationship… How are we doing, sweetie? Are you stuck in a funnel…? Let's review them, and see if there's any funnel-type set up.

..............................................................................................................

..............................................................................................................

..............................................................................................................

..............................................................................................................

## ◎ KEY TAKEAWAYS

★ The real damage in an abusive relationship is not just the actions they take, but the deliberate act of dragging you into your own insecurities and instability.

★ "Emotional Manipulation" is a combination of confusing elements like deliberate ambiguity, gaslighting, and emotional withholding.

★ They use a "Triple Slap Technique," which includes "Direct Damage" (humiliation, disappearing) and "Avoidance Damage" (blame-shifting, future-faking) to avoid accountability.

★ "Funnel Agreements" are a key tool where they have freedom while restricting yours, revealing their own insecurities.

★ The confusion you feel is not a side effect, but the actual result of their manipulation.

# FROM DISASTER TO MEH: A QUEER SCALE OF DISTRESS

*"The subconscious mind automates processes in order to save energy"*

Ugh… After the last two chapters, and before we move on, I need to share some light with you…

Probably, if you are reading this book, you have many "WTFs" in your head. Over time, this relationship has made you accumulate painful events, and at the same time loose strength, so it's totally normal to have our nervous system on high alert, to feel anxiety or even fear. And I know (very well) that sometimes the nervous system will get totally altered for *"just an intuition."* Probably generated by their breadcrumb path…

I remember that I got to a point where I was living in anxiety and I didn't know what to do to stop my head from spinning.

We need to learn how to control that. Or at least, how to do better. So we are going to learn (Spaniard coming…) *"How to Stop*

*Spiralizing"* (Yes... that's how I always used that word, without understanding the smiles I would receive back...!).

I want to share a tool that changed the game for me in the last stages of my turd. I mean "my relationship" but I don't like to say that, cos it was never *mine...* you get me....

Before we move on: **What you are suffering is real. *The whole* dynamic and events that you are living in is abuse. Some specific events or behaviors are directly abusive. This tool doesn't mean to minimize the reality of what we are living now or we lived in a past relationship.**

I have to thank Rafael Santandreu for his books. They inspired me to adapt this beautiful tool to this specific situation and to *us*. Please, don't underestimate it.

We are going to use it with separate and specific events (one by one, darling). With all those minor/major aggressions that trigger us almost daily... or actually, just daily. Having our nervous system under control allows us to think more clearly and also feel better. We want that, right?

**Welcome to the Scale of Disaster:**

| PERFECTION | GREAT! | PRETTY GOOD | | ACTUALLY, BAD | VERY BAD | DISASTER |

The world doesn't teach any of us (queer or not) how to live in the gray zone. We are taught to polarize our emotions. So we consider that all the bad things that happen are terrible, or a disaster, and that all the good is Perfection! We are not trained to locate the events in the grey zone.

Why are you worried that PS has disappeared? Have you noticed that all the time you are spiralizing because *"PS might be doing…"* you are actually not doing anything yourself?

When I started using this tool, I saw that I could spend hours in spirals. Soon I started to see that there is a whole world in front of me, full of joy. **My joy.** not joy motivated by revenge. I started focusing on doing things that brought me joy instead of giving my time and attention to someone else. And guess what? PS started to feel insecure, because there wasn't the expected supply.

Imagine when we suddenly see a good friend on the streets. *"Aaaah!"* Right? We react like we just won the lottery! (And actually, a good friend is a lottery prize, but let's take a look at the way we react). Imagine when we get that *good call*, we were waiting for. *"Aaaah!"* Again, the perfect event that *made my day*.

Now, imagine when we are carrying a six-pack of beer, and the box breaks. The beer didn't make it. *"Fuck!"* Tax day… *"FUCK…"* Bills, gossip, you name it, everything is terrible.

So, inside our mind, we live like this, ping-ponging between the two sides of the scale:

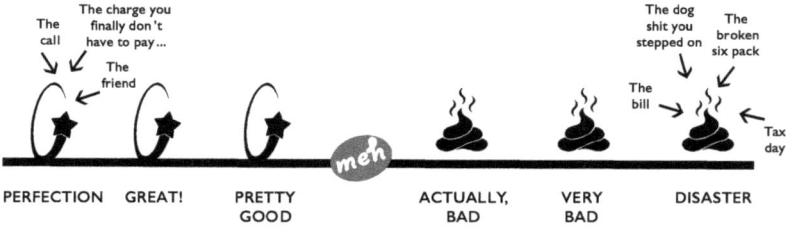

Now this is key: Supported by several psychological and neuroscientific models, it's known that **we first think** (consciously or subconsciously) and **then we feel**. Based on how we feel, we behave (take actions).

So, when we face events, our brain quickly **thinks**, *"Perfection! Or Disaster?"* Based on that answer, it will trigger certain **emotions**, and depending how we feel, we'll start jumping for joy, or we'll be pissed off.

Our subconscious is so wired to interpret bad as terrible and good as perfect, that we do it in self-drive mode... We don't even have time to evaluate properly! Our brain has already done it, so we need to learn to insert this technique when we feel that pinch in the stomach.

But now, let me throw some turds down here, and let's think objectively together:

- You are ignored by PS
- PS lied to you
- And had sex with...
- You are discarded
- You are publicly humiliated
- You receive a mean answer from PS
- PS is not answering the phone
- PS might be... (intuitions and breadcrumbs)

Considering what you are dealing with from PS, and extracting the specific events that compound the abuse (which I think is *"Very Bad"*), add a few turds yourself. List things that trigger you pretty often.

......................................................... .........................................................

......................................................... .........................................................

What could be *"Perfection!"* events? Winning the lottery? Getting a castle from a European uncle you didn't even know? Meeting your true self from higher dimensions?? Think with me! What could be a **perfect** life event?

..................................................................................

..................................................................................

What could be *"Great!"*? To find a new career path? To meet someone special? Think about a few examples that resonate with you.

..................................................................................

..................................................................................

What could be *"Pretty Good"*? To meet a nice new person? To find ten bucks on the ground? What could be pretty good for you... objectively!

..................................................................................

..................................................................................

What could be *"Meh..."*? To not find the brand of creamer you like in the supermarket? Let's go for it, what is it for you?

..................................................................................

..................................................................................

Now let's get into the dark area... What could be actually bad? OBJECTIVELY! To have your car at the workshop for repairs? Is it... *"Actually Bad"*? Or is it nearer *"Meh..."*? Getting unexpectedly fired? For me is bad, but I could always find another one so it's not terrible. What would be *"Actually Bad"* for you?

..................................................................................

..................................................................................

*"Very Bad"*, for me, I think it would be something like losing a limb. I know you can have a great life afterwards, but the event and

the work to accept a new reality and move on happily, would be a lot for me. Let's get raw... What would it be for you?

.................................................. ..................................................................
.................................................. ..................................................................

Objectively!

I think, something like getting a diagnosis saying I have two weeks left of life would be a terrible event. A *"Disaster."* The joy I feel trying to support my community and people going through what I did feels like a purpose, and I want to do it as long as possible. Let's go to the end of the scale, where you cannot go lower. There's nothing worse (in your actual understanding) that could happen. What is it?

.................................................................................................................
.................................................................................................................

So, objectively my internal scale should look like this:

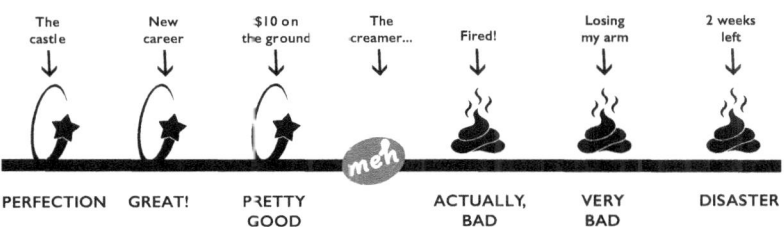

Now, let's fill it up with your own examples on the empty scale below (stick with me...). This is your own scale:

**Please remember:** This is not about saying what happened wasn't bad. It's about perspective, about giving your brain a break from seeing everything as a 'disaster,' which drains your energy)

255

## Sweetie-pie's internal scale:

**Your name** .................................................

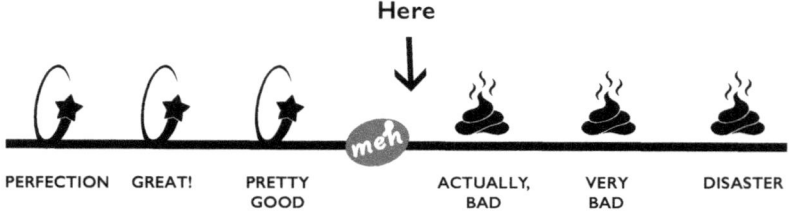

| PERFECTION | GREAT! | PRETTY GOOD | | ACTUALLY, BAD | VERY BAD | DISASTER |

Okay, now that we have everything ready, the magic begins...

What if most of our daily struggles are here?:

**Here**

↓

| PERFECTION | GREAT! | PRETTY GOOD | | ACTUALLY, BAD | VERY BAD | DISASTER |

Not nice... maybe not even normal, but let's say, objectively they are "a little bit bad."

One of the problems we face is that many of the behaviors of PS become *triggers*, because of an accumulation of pain while losing strength, because of traumatic experiences, and because we have gone through it so many times that our brain has *"automated the path."* So now, our brain has learnt and automated the path, the process of thinking is bypassed, and we either get directly to feelings or even reactions. The whole process is sped up and our brain knows what we normally do, so it bypasses the feelings (they'll come right after reacting, you know that...).

I want you to be specific with me, but first, let me throw some turds down here. Let's place the next events in the scale by using comparison, **objectively** in your own scale above (some of them are worse than others):

- You are ignored by PS
- PS lied to you
- And had sex with…
- Gaslighting (choose a recent event)
- You are publicly humiliated
- That bad answer
- PS is not answering the phone
- PS might be… (intuitions and breadcrumbs)
- PS is on the apps…

Thinking about what you are dealing with with PS and extracting the most specific events that compound the abuse (which I think is *"Very Bad"* or worse), add a few turds yourself, things that trigger you pretty often:

..................................................................................................................

..................................................................................................................

..................................................................................................................

So imagine that, for you, *"Actually Bad"* is to get fired,. How bad is it when someone like PS, who regularly manipulates you and ignores you, ignores you or doesn't answer the phone? Is it as bad as getting fired? Is it actually *"a little bit bad"*? Is it *"Disaster"*?

Ask these questions with every turd before deciding where to put it on the scale.

Have you done it? Come on… I want you to see it graphically, so the image will stick in your memory. We want that…

How many of the turds (mine and yours) have you located near *"Meh…"*? How many turds have you located near or on *"Actually Bad"*? And, how many turds have you located as worse than *"Actually Bad"*?

Please remember, we are working with specific events to deal with them better. We are not categorizing the resulting *abuse*.

For me, and most of the people I work with, it looks something like:

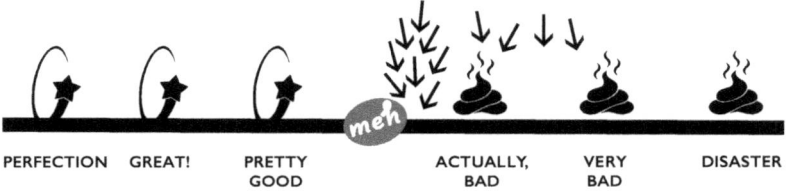

| PERFECTION | GREAT! | PRETTY GOOD | | ACTUALLY, BAD | VERY BAD | DISASTER |

What does yours look like? I want you to look at your own scale for a few seconds.

*Now, WTF are we doing, Daniel?!*

**We are thinking.** Thinking away from triggers. Thinking bit by bit. Now that we understand what we are into, it's time to learn how to navigate better, until we completely break free. If every time something happens we go to the bigger picture—*"I'm in an abusive relationship"*—or our wonderful brain simply puts everything in the section *"Disaster"* because of triggers, our influences, and so on, then coping with a person like PS until we go zero contact is pretty undigestible. So we cut the steak into smaller pieces in order to chew better and digest better…

## Thinking - Feeling - Acting

By actively changing the first step, by using this tool, we are changing the whole sequence! This could move you from taking action impulsively (the goal of PS) to taking time to be strategic or just calm.

The fact that you can place many of the events from *"Disaster"* to near *"Meh…"* **is giving you power.** What PS is doing, is cooking Froggie very slowly. Small events that drain you and over time weaken you, with some bigger slaps in the middle. What PS doesn't know is how much Froggie is learning…

How would this look in action?

Normally, we get awareness in the "Feeling" stage, so let's use "Feelings" as an alert.

Imagine that tomorrow you go to the supermarket and there's no more creamer for your coffee, and you start feeling upset or angry… *Alert!*

Where should this event (no creamer) be on my scale? Just a little worse than *"Meh…"*. So, every time the feeling comes back, just say *"Meh…"*, or it's just a little bit bad. By doing this, we are going back to that *"too automatic process"* called *thinking*, and consciously re-doing it.

PS doesn't reply to a text… My brain is saying *"Disaster."* But I think about it and I see that the specific event of PS not answering my messages is *"Meh… just annoying…"* I start feeling better, so instead of turning on the detective mode (powered by the need to find evidences, so I can prove to myself and PS that I'm not wrong or *"crazy"*… Does this sound familiar?), I choose to go for a swim because I have the beach near by. Staying out of the *"Disaster"* range allows me to take different actions.

You don't have to do anything else. The rest of the process will be created by your brain so you will feel better and take better actions.

There will be events that will be "less bad," and other times when you will get pissed off because it's actually too much, and that's okay. But you now have a filter that will allow you to engage less, and focus your energy on yourself.

When I first tried the Scale of Disaster, I remember I got angry. It was a very dark time for me. I was constantly researching about the mind and about relationships and I used to say (and I still think the same): *Why do I have to collapse, in order to find proven resources that work!? Why is this not taught in schools? Why don't we have proper mental health education?* How many hard situations would I have handled way better if I had known this at a young age? Things like harmful comments from straight people because I was gay. I could've been able to say *"Meh... you don't even deserve my attention!"*

One of my life purposes is to help promote mental health education as a subject. I don't know how, but it's in my list of dreams I'll fight for.

This tool to stop "spiralizing" has helped thousands of people to cope better in life and in their relationships. Please, please, please, try it...

## ♕ ACTION STEPS

Meet me in the next QR…. Today we will work together!

## 🎯 KEY TAKEAWAYS

★ Your nervous system can be constantly on alert from daily triggers, causing you to "spiralize" and lose energy.

★ The "Scale of Disaster" is a tool to help you reframe events and stop polarizing your emotions into *"Perfection!"* or *"Disaster!"*

★ By consciously re-thinking an event and placing it on a scale from *"Meh..."* to *"Disaster,"* you can break the automatic "thinking-feeling-acting" cycle.

★ Using this tool allows you to engage less with the narcissist and take better, more strategic actions that focus on yourself.

★ The goal is to move many of the narcissist's behaviors from *"Disaster"* into the *"Meh..."* category, which gives you back power and energy.

# HACKER MODE ON™

Darling, from the moment you understand where you are, believe me, you have to navigate…

**From now on…**

The moment you see the trap, different things **should** happen:

- If you are manipulated on a regular basis, you don't need to speak your truth. That person doesn't deserve your honesty, not even you sharing big news.

- The agreements on your side, you know: don't hurt, don't initiate a war, and don't get in trouble… but do your thing. Find things that bring you joy, meet people, just make sure you don't fall into *"if PS fucks, I fuck."* Look inside and see what you truly want to do. Stop restricting your freedom for them. You don't owe them loyalty.

- The tools you have now to identify what's happening (seeing the PS's Bar Classic Combos) can help you see, and from seeing, we go to handling. **Who is in the trap now?**

In the meantime, we will provide *"Fake Supply."* [Coming Soon]

## NARCI-BOX™

*Your new toolbox for not too long…*

### Disarming Narci-Questions™ and Narci-Forms™ (Use via text message only)

I want to give you a type of question you can use to confirm, get evidence, and (try to) protect your freedom, until you finally say *bye!*

*"So, is it okay that I do it?*
*If you say that's normal, then I can do it too, right?*
*No drama."*

Get ready for the drama, baby. This is where they are going to activate all the tools. So they will answer something like:

*"I don't want us to do anything to hurt each other."*
*"I don't want to label something that hurt you as normal."*

And here's where we take them back to the corner:

*"Oh, I'm not hurt. I'm not complaining about what you did. The question is still the same.*
*If you say that's normal, then is it okay for me to do it?"*

Here you might be able to get a little bit of truth or validation:

*"Okay, what I did was not nice, I see it now… but now I know! It will not happen again!"*

Here we can see an example of Non-Apology + Blame-Shifting.

**Non-Apology:** They are not naming the pain, even if they said sorry, they'd be avoiding. To make it fully work they add "Poetic-Blame-Shifting."

**Blame-Shifting:** *"I don't want to label as "normal" something that hurts you."* Sweetie pie STOP JUICING, you're gonna get dehydrated. This may sounds kind of nice, BUT they are saying that the problem is that whatever happened hurts **you**. Never the fact they caused the damage. *"I see it now,"* bravo... the game of *"I didn't know,"* do you know that it actually means *"you didn't communicate clearly enough?"* Also, after feeling cornered and not showing any intentions to even name the damage, this is the fastest way out: *"I didn't know but now I know, so now let's put the shit in the drawer, reset life, blame you over time...!"*

Don't get blinded by poetic manipulation, they should be accountable without your massive efforts, period.

That's not even admitting the truth, so please don't get hooked by it. To get there, you have spent hours of your life redirecting their manipulation...

Don't let that validation feeling win inside you. They are admitting **a small percentage** of the truth, just to give you what you need. The second part of the sentence is focuses on *"don't do the same"* while they already did it. And this will be just one more loop in your life... (Funnel-Agreements). We are not disarming to feel better in the relationship.

Narci-Forms™ are the evolution of the Narci-Questions™. You can adapt this template and simply copy-paste it into your life. Again, we don't need the real answers, we just need evidence of manipulation.

- Is it okay that I do the same? Or would it hurt you?

- If it's okay, great. We adapt our agreements. But if it hurts you, why are you defending it?

- If it would hurt you, why don't you simply apologize?

- If it would hurt you, why are you framing it as *"normal"*?

**The goal of these techniques is observation, confirmation, and gathering evidence that will weigh more than our trauma bonding. It's not about learning to deal with manipulation better in order to stay.**

**Note:** These tools can lead to a never-ending loop. Instead of accepting anything, PS will keep trying to manipulate. Remember, the goal is not to win — it's to confirm and clearly see the manipulation. The moment you need the loop to stop, simply tell them they're right. (Yes, it can be that simple…)

## Your New Superpower

*Detective Mode™: when your sparkle turns into a flashlight,  and your heart becomes a forensic lab.*

We have expanded our intelligence by perfecting our *"Detective Mode™,"* but we know that's a trap that gets tighter. The better you get at it, the more sophisticated it becomes.

So I'm going to gift you with your new superpower:

## Indifference

At the beginning, it can be very hard, but believe me, you can get very good at it… and you know what you'll finally find? The tap that controls the *supply*.

**[emoji sunglasses]**

*"The opposite of love is not hate, it is indifference."*

Think about it: hating requires energy. It activates your nervous system and pulls you into visceral feelings. All that energy spent is a gift, is some kind of *"behind-the-curtain-on-going-supply,"* for *PS*, even when you fake indifference but you still feel the rage.

The real next level is when you don't even care, when you understand that the time invested in playing that game where you try to make a bottle land vertically, is way, way, way better than planning to hit the ON button of the "Detective Mode"…

This indifference should never sound like, *"Don't worry, it's okay, I don't mind"* with an upset tone of voice… That is supply, and they know you're actually angry. They matter.

The concentrated force of this superpower sounds like this. Let me share a classic:

After they disappear, as a way to make you feel discarded, they will call you. This time, probably you won't hear the phone ringing. Couple texts… missed. Oops! They will think you are angry and you aren't answering on purpose when suddenly… YOU CALL BACK.

**[In a good-mood voice:"**

**[Me]** *"Hi, hon! Scrry, I was in the shower and I didn't hear the phone. How are you?"*

[PS's Head] *Shower? Having sex? Going out? He's not angry?? What has he been doing while I thought he was crying over me?!*

The next step? They'll try to fill the gaps — and now they're falling into their own trap. They're the ones needing to KNOW.

[PS] *"I'm good… What have you been doing?"*

Here they are feeling insecure, and at the same time they are still testing your mood. They want you angry. They know you know they did something wrong…

[Me] *I've been great! I went for a walk… enjoyed the sun… did some work… you know, here and there, but doing great!* **[Sweetie, why not a little touch of wishy washy, right?]**

[PS's Head] *Wait, what?* Now's when I was supposed to get my attention, my supply… Where is it?

And stick with me because this is the best part of the classic:

Next, PS will generate a problem. Any word, any microtone, anything will be enough to start drama. They need supply, so they'll provoke you — to make you react or lower your shield so they can see what's truly behind…

[Me, answering provocation] *Hey, what are you doing? Are you okay? 'Cause I just told you I'm doing great… Look, let's talk later, okay? Have fun.*

Instead of engaging, just a touch of exposing *"what are you doing?"* using a nice, calm and happy tone… At this point, the best thing is to cut the conversation short.

**[PS's Head]** *Wait, what? You don't want to know what I did??? You are not going to show yourself as controlling, even though I just gave you possible evidence of crossing one of our boundaries?? Do you not care???!*

Do you know how all this *Classic Combo* cycle also translates?:

**Your happiness makes them angry.**

**[PS's Head]** *Challenge created. I'm going to do it again, but this time it is gonna itch.*

**[My head and also your head]:** *Don't worry, baby, because we're ready to simply be ourselves, a smiley, nice person who wants to live in a peaceful state of mind. So, at the second wave, we'll use our superpower again, as many times as necessary.*

Is it easy? No. Is it worth it? Yes. **You are cutting supply**, the reason why the relationship is alive.

Once they perceive no supply, they start to feel that feeling that is familiar for you, *"this relationship isn't working."* The difference is that you are dealing with trauma bonding, struggling to go, and they will just be ready to say *"Byeee"*.

Every successful use of this superpower weakens not PS, but the damn trauma bonding that is making it hard for you to leave.

## Fake Supply

Yes… you'll soon know precisely **when** they need supply… And you also know how to use indifference…

But what if…

...that weekend when you were ignored... *when you seemed so affected...*

**you actually had a great time?**

...and they don't even know how... who with... why... I think... **they should never know it was actually good!**

**[Emoji Sunglasses]**

You can expand your freedom without weaponizing it, and without letting the alarms in PS activate...
    No more explanation needed... right?


**Nearby Profiles ON - Travel Mode OFF**

Do you know what they're doing while you're investigating, with your anxiety levels hitting the roof?

**Enjoying life.**

Do you know what you're not doing while you're investigating?

**Enjoying life.**

And you know what?

**Nobody deserves to own of your time or your joy.**

We need to start this process:

*What would bring **me** joy on this solo Saturday night?*

Okay, now mark everything you think you want, just because PS might be doing it.

And now look at the list of what you really want. You, without the influence of the uncertainty generated against you.

And now, guess what? **Go do it.**

Once you truly understand that you're not giving that power to anyone… **your power begins.**

[Emoji sunglasses]

## The Kryptonite for Your Powers

Before discarding you, believe me, they will try to get supply somehow. And the key to opening that door is your **empathy.** They'll try to figure out what has changed by love bombing you.

[My head and also your head]: *Don't worry baby. Now we know.*

Once you start using your power without the commitment to leave, you might start crossing the lines of your own identity. It's one thing to use it to navigate, to control your mind without giving yourself away, but it's another thing entirely to do what they do. To use insecurity against someone.

Don't use this superpowers to provoke or for revenge. Just to disengage.

**Note:** These are not techniques to delay leaving or to generate pain. The underlying truth here is that you're suffering, and it's fair to navigate your situation until you leave. It's fair to play within the real terms of your relationship's dynamic.

With tools like fake supply or practicing indifference, you can actually start moving the needle... for the first time!

These tools won't work from the moment you reveal them, so be careful!

But there's one more tool... to use your extreme analytical capacity... to get a second brain.

## Welcome to Narci-AI™

## [Look inside the next QR code!]

**Note:** This tool does not replace professional therapy, is not meant to diagnose, and is not a substitute for real human support. It's simply an emergency resource, for that moment when the whole world is asleep and your mind won't stop spinning. Use it with common sense. Let it be your emotional flashlight in the dark.

## ◎ KEY TAKEAWAYS

☆ Your new superpower is **Indifference**, which you can use to cut off their supply and stop their game.

☆ Indifference is the opposite of love, as hate still requires energy and gives the narcissist supply.

☆ You can "fake" indifference by staying calm, joyful, and non-reactive. It makes them feel powerless and insecure.

☆ Disarming Narci-Questions™ and Narci-Forms™ are a tools to confirm their manipulative behavior and gain evidence.

## ✕ YOU MUST NOT USE THESE TOOLS TO STAY IN THE RELATIONSHIP.

**Find your Third Superpower, Narci-AI™ and more...**

www.thesparkletrap.com/qr3

# BACK TO CHAPTER 8 –
# DEVALUATION SECTION

(page 55)